Jail House Cuisine

From the Right Side of the Bars

D1210613

Louise Mathews

outskirtspress

DENVER, COLORADO

[handwritten inscription]

Jail House Cuisine
From the Right Side of the Bars
All Rights Reserved.
Copyright © 2015 Louise Mathews
v3.0

Outskirts Press, Inc.
http://www.outskirtspress.com

ISBN: 978-1-4787-4716-1

Library of Congress Control Number: 2014956618

Outskirts Press and the "OP" logo are trademarks belonging to Outskirts Press, Inc.

PRINTED IN THE UNITED STATES OF AMERICA

We may live without poetry, music and art

We may live without conscience and love without heart

We may live without friends, we may live without books

But civilized man cannot live without cooks

—Owen Wister (1860-1938)

This book is dedicated to all the wonderful and professional food service staff of the San Diego Sheriff's Department who worked with me from 1986-2007. Their loyalty to the department, dedication to their duties, ultimate professionalism and tremendous skills resulted in the best Correctional Food Service in the Country. Thanks to all of you, we were able to accomplish our goals and realize our dreams. With gratitude and love....LM

Table of Contents

A Word About the Recipes i

Prologue v

Introduction vii

Chapter 1:   Before God Made Man 1

Chapter 2:   Going Behind Bars 15

Chapter 3:   First Day Shock 21

Chapter 4:   Now for the Second Week 32

Chapter 5:   And Then There Was More 44

Chapter 6:   San Diego Goes Modern; A Dream Come True 59

Chapter 7:   This and That 69

Chapter 8:   The Young, the Not So Young and the Special 84

Chapter 9:   Cooking with Conviction 97

Chapter 10: New Orleans 103

Chapter 11: Down South 109

Chapter 12: Middle of the Country and Further Out North 123

Chapter 13: Way Out West 133

Chapter 14: Get Out of Town 147

Chapter 15: One Can Always Use Good "PR" 160

Chapter 16: Always Have Fun 172

Index of Recipes 177

About the Author 181

A Word About the Recipes

These are some of the things you should know about the recipes presented here. When I started writing this book I was only going to have a few recipes in it to give you an idea about what it is like to eat in jail. But once I got going I could see that I needed to add more so that you would get a better, more complete picture. You may even find yourself outside of San Diego in jail so I thought I would go worldwide.

I had a heck of a time getting recipes from my peers who are the Food Service Managers and Directors for Corrections throughout the world. Most people were surprised that anyone would be interested in the food served in jail. I asked them to think about which recipes their inmates and staff liked the most so some of them did.

I have endeavored to have recipes from different parts of the country and a few from other countries as well. Believe it or not, I found more similarities than differences. I didn't even ask institutions for recipes if I would not eat their food; in some jails, I wouldn't even sit down, never mind eat! So…you have only <u>the best of the best</u>.

Things to remember:

- Food Service Managers in jails have a tight budget, therefore the ingredients are all very simple and easy to find. (Yes, you can find alligator if you look for it)
- We use the KISS method (keep it simple stupid) as a lot of the cooking is done by unskilled inmates. Therefore, these recipes are basically simple and easy to do as well as delicious.
- Most of the food in jail is made from scratch and is healthier than in most places. The larger jails tend to cook food by steaming, baking or broiling, not frying. A large number of jails, including San Diego, cook as "heart healthy" as possible.

- Since hot cooked cereals and all kinds of bean dishes and soups from scratch are easy and inexpensive for us to make, these items tend to be served almost all over the country. Guess what? They are good for you.

- I asked the Food Service Directors of other jails for recipes to feed the smallest amount of people they had. The range of portions per recipe I received was from <u>50-4,000</u> portions per recipe. I had to cut them down to feed 6-8 people, trying all the while to keep the authenticity of each one, and then test it to death. The desserts were fun (some were tested many times) but some of the others were a challenge to say the least. Some of the recipes gave me a list of ingredients with no cooking instructions and vice-versa and some were very precise. I have included a few original recipes along with the finished ones so you can see the process I had to use and what I went through, just for you.

- The type and size of the cooking equipment in institutional kitchens is much different than in our homes. Since we all use some kind of steam kettle in jails, you will find that I use a pressure cooker in some recipes to better simulate the kettle cooking. Also, the kinds of equipment you use have a lot to do with how the recipe tastes and looks. For instance, the Ranger Cookies from San Diego will taste and look a little different from the ones served in jail but you will still know what they are if you ever become a guest.

- Today's Restaurant Chefs are all very fond of the "Farm to Fork" method of preparing meals. I am here to tell you that jails have been doing that for hundreds of years. Many institutions have their own gardens and fruit trees, cattle and chicken farms and dairies. You can't get more "farm to fork" than that, yes? On top of that it is sometimes organic and free-range; are we modern all ready or what? It is nice to know we are in style!

I had various testers; the chief ones were Larry, my patient husband, most of my family and my dear friend Karen and her mom Maureen who tasted *almost* everything. I can't tell you how much I appreciated their assistance; I could not have done it without them! A special note of thanks goes to my daughter, Michelle Lein, for providing sketches and artistic advice in the design of the book cover.

For the main part, if you should go to jail in California or Michigan or Porto Rico or Ontario, Canada or Alabama you will be familiar with the food and that is part of my goal. You will have enough unique experiences during your incarceration without one of them being the food.

If you have any comments or questions about the recipes, please do not hesitate to log on to my face book page and I will be glad to help you. I wish you good cooking and good eating but please try to stay on the "Right Side of the Bars".

Prologue

I stood there looking up at the ten story building, not ready to go in just yet. At first glance, it was nothing special; tan colored and streaked with brown downtown soot. But looking up past the second story, the iron barred windows stood out from the face of the building, giving it an ominous air. The bars ran all the way up to the flat topped roof with a rim of what looked like a wire cage.

Even though it was a perfect late summer day in San Diego, with the temperature hovering at 72 degrees, I could feel the sweat trickling down my back. I was praying it didn't show through my dress. I had dressed carefully for what would be the last interview for a position with the Sheriff. I was hoping that my light blue shirtwaist dress with a wide belt, pearl necklace and plain black two inch heeled pumps, would pass muster for a job in the jails.

It had taken me the better part of a year to get to this point yet I stood frozen in place, staring at the two doors which led into the building. I knew that the door on the right went into the jail itself and the door on the left went to the Sheriff's administration offices.

Today I was going through the left door, the less scary of the two. But I was still anxious, my mind going over all the horrible stories I had heard about what happens behind bars.

What was a nice girl like me doing here, willingly planning to work in jails? This girl needed a good-paying steady position so....I gathered up my courage, stepped around the vagrants lounging in front of the jail, and turned the handle.

Introduction

Kissing don't last! Cookery do!
—*George Meredith*

I had the good fortune to work for the San Diego, California Sheriff's Department as their Chief of Food and Nutrition Services for almost 21 years. Upon my retirement in 2007, an article written by Karen Weisberg in Foodservice Director Magazine, for the Legends feature, entitled *Correctional Chieftain*, went a long way in summing up my career. Karen wrote, 'Throughout her 21 year career in San Diego, Louise Mathews has tenaciously and successfully fought to improve jail food and its public perception.'

Providing good food in jail was a big fight but I did not know how almost impossible it was at the time. From the beginning, I set out to change the mind set people had about jail food. I was young and thought I was invincible and could do anything I envisioned. I came to realize many of the correctional administrators, food service staff and even the public did not agree with me; after all, they were "only inmates". Whenever anyone said that it made my blood boil!

Make no mistake; I am not a "bleeding heart". I believe people who do the crime must do the time but it doesn't negate the fact that inmates are human beings with civil rights. The meals served to them must be as good as we could make them under the circumstances. I could not do anything but my best and I knew I could change the way things were done, if only in the facilities I was responsible for or for the ones for which I provided consulting services.

With the support of the Sheriff's command staff and my excellent foodservice team we succeeded in many ways. We built a Central Production Center where we cooked and packaged all the food for the

County. We used new technology called Cook/Chill. Simply put, this is a method of food production where you cook the food and then chill it down quickly to below 40 degrees. The food can then be stored safely in refrigeration for as long as 4-6 weeks. Most major restaurant chains were already using this procedure with great success.

97% of the riots in Corrections are over food; when they riot, buildings burn down and people get hurt or killed. Due to the managed way we produced and served meals, *there was not one riot or lawsuit over food in 21 years.* We were awarded every top award there is in the Foodservice Industry including receiving the Diamond Award as the best Correctional Foodservice in the country.

People from all over the world came to observe us; not only Corrections but hospitals, hotels and restaurants. Many of them returned to their facilities and built new kitchens and production centers, copying what we were doing. We trained many food service administrators and cooks in our facility; my staff loved sharing their skills and experience. It felt so good to be emulated and appreciated and it showed in the moral of our staff.

During the time that I was Chief of Food Services for the Sheriff I continued my consulting work and I am still doing so. I am an Operational, Management and Design Consultant, specializing in the correctional field. From 1990 to the present, I was involved in the design and operation of several production centers. My clients ranged from New Orleans to Montana to Canada to California to Chicago. I even had an opportunity to assist the Marine Corps with their facility in Japan.

I love assisting people with their new projects; my friends say that I love spending other people's money. It was even more fun when these people got it all back in spades when they realized cost savings along with increased sanitation and quality control. There is immense satisfaction when you assist others in making their dreams come true.

I did not *ever* aspire to work in the jails or be involved in law enforcement. Many people have asked me if I was afraid to work in jails. I tell them I grew up on the streets of Brooklyn and quickly learned to be aware of those around me and to walk like I was not afraid of anyone. Besides, in jail you absolutely know who the bad people are and not so much the people on the street.

It turned out to be the best thing that ever happened to me and I enjoyed it immensely. The purpose of this book is to share some of my experiences with you as well as some good recipes. It is also meant to prepare you for jail if you ever find yourself on the wrong side of the bars.

I got the idea for this book when a reporter did a story on the Sheriff's Food Service and ran it in the food section of the newspaper. The article was titled *Justice Serves* by Caroline Dipping, published August 3, 2005, in the San Diego Union; it is one of the best articles written about our Food Service.

To quote from the article, 'Louise Mathews makes sure that those behind bars get some decent grub. Beet salad; Yuck! Pineapple sauce on the ham; Fuhgeddaboudit! You may think that your family is a tough crowd to please, but consider Louise Mathews' job. For 19 years she has been cooking up three squares a day for a discriminating-albeit captive-audience of thousands.'

Caroline had it in a nutshell. One of the most difficult things about this job is the necessity to satisfy as many of the 9 year old to 104 year old inmates I fed each day as possible. Food is one of the most important things to an inmate; what will it be like, when do I get fed, will there be choices? These are some of the first thoughts an inmate has when entering the system. Some of the worst offenders; rapists, murderers and child molesters, actually worry about someone in the kitchen trying to poison them. (Now why would anyone want to do that?)

We provided meals to over 8,000 inmates and staff per day which is a tall order. When you throw in the tight budget, special medical and religious diets and strict regulations, it became gargantuan! For instance, I thought that the beet salad tasted great and it also satisfied many of the vitamin requirements for the day. But the inmates hated it and wouldn't eat it. It doesn't do any good unless they actually eat it so I took it off the menu.

They also didn't much like the pineapple sauce on the ham but I made it less sweet and left it on the menu because it kept the ham moist in the heating process and they finally got to like it. I told the kitchen inmate workers that it was gourmet food and they spread that around to the other inmates; see what a little gossip can do?

It wasn't the first time we were in a publication but this was a long article, complete with recipes. Since I fed the reporter and photographer all the different kinds of food we were preparing that day, they insisted on the recipes being included in the article.

For a few years after it was published, people would stop me, some of them strangers, and tell me that they had "jail house food night" for their families and that they loved it. So, when I got ready to embark on my new writing career, I thought I would start with a jail house cook book so you all can have your own "jail house food night".

Would you believe that we actually received compliments and requests for our recipes from inmates? I cannot tell you how many times I have been approached on the street by former inmates as well as inmates in other jail and prison facilities, who thanked me for the good food we gave them in San Diego. Of course, they knew me and I had no idea who *they* were which is kind of scary if you think about it. However, it was high praise indeed!

In the beginning, I was going to include just our recipes in San Diego. However, I realized that people all over the country and even the world would be reading this book so I decided to include other states and some other countries as well. I have tried to give the reader a good view of what it is like behind bars. I have personally been in most of the jail systems I have included in the book or at least know the Food Service folks who were the contributors.

I would not recommend going to jail in many of our states as some places are better than others if you find yourself incarcerated. California is the most liberal state and one of the strictest in its regulations concerning housing and food service so it is my first choice.

In some states, many jails are not air conditioned and vermin of all kinds share your cell. I was visiting some jails in the South and I learned that if I kept moving, the ants wouldn't crawl up my legs. The inmates were all lying on the concrete floors in order to be able to breathe better in the heat while their lunch bags sat on the window sill for hours in the sun where the bugs were smart enough not to go.

Some states have chain gangs and work for hours in the heat while inmates in other states sit in air conditioned comfort, watching TV and work only if they want to or can qualify for assignments. As you can see, there is no one *typical* jail scenario; you take your chances, depending on where you go to jail.

It is the same in other countries. For instance, be good and try not to get arrested when you go to Mexico where they do not believe in feeding you; you have to have people bring food in for you. What they do give you, if anything, I have heard is not edible. At least we feed people in the U.S.

There is a jail in Great Britain that is a brand new six story building, light and bright with lots of windows. This is unusual since a lot of jails are solid concrete buildings with slits for windows. The cells are private one man cells that look like a small hotel room with a bench type bed with storage underneath, a wall mounted TV, book shelves and a desk and chair. There is a large, fully stocked weight room, a huge indoor basket ball court, a badminton court in an outdoor activity area and an indoor recreation room with game tables, an exercise bike and TV.

Food served here was "pretty good" but boring; at least it was prepared with top of the line sanitation and safety controls. Of course, you still don't have your freedom to leave the facility but what a way to do your time!

Compare this to the other end of the spectrum; the Correctional facility in the Republic of Palau. It is in a group of islands between Guam and the Philippines. The jail housed 97 inmates, both men and women. They were in for anywhere from six months to life. They had only one inmate cook, Justin, who was originally from Guam but who had spent time in Missouri working for restaurants and received some dietary training at a long term facility.

This turned out to be a blessing as there was not much to work with in this jail. There was no set menu, standards or guidelines. The food was what was available or was donated; mainly canned fish and noodles. The kitchen was a small, old "house like" galley kitchen with most of the cooking done in two crock-like vessels.

The refrigerator didn't work and was used to store pots and pans. The rats were as big as cats and were a serious problem along with a lack of sanitation due to budget cuts to buy cleaning supplies. When one person got sick, almost everyone else did as well.

A typical menu was pancakes and syrup for breakfast and ramen type noodles with canned tuna, sardines or mackerel for lunch and dinner. That was it; no bread, fruit, beverages or desserts. Believe me; I would really behave myself on that island! Needless to say, I have not supplied a recipe for you from this facility.

On the other hand, some historic jails have been turned into haute hotels; they draw those people who have always wondered what it was like to be incarcerated. In Boston, Beacon Hill's Charles Street Jail, which once housed the Boston Strangler and Malcolm X, was renovated to the tune of one hundred and fifty million dollars and is now called the Liberty Hotel. Its topaz-hued lobby incorporates the original brick walls while historic catwalks link up to an open lobby and some jail cells still remain in the street level bar. I would love to see it but I definitely wouldn't sleep there! I have seen enough of jails, even a jail they fancied up.

Please note this is the story of my life in the food service industry, especially of my time spent working in jails from 1986-2007, to the best of my recollection. Some names and places have been changed to protect the *guilty* as well as the innocent. Come join me for a new and interesting experience to see what eating can be like on the wrong side of the bars.

❦❦❦

CREAM OF BROCCOLI SOUP (Serves 6-8)

This soup was an absolute favorite with the inmates and staff. In fact, I received several comments and requests for the recipe over the years. One female inmate wrote: 'I have visited your establishment several times and I have always enjoyed the Broccoli Soup. I have been here for almost a month and I haven't seen it yet. When can I expect it to be on my menu?'

She was right; it was off the menu for a while. I had received a lot of canned asparagus through the commodity program and we were making cream of asparagus soup with it at a lower cost. This is what I wrote her back: 'Broccoli is out of season and asparagus is in so you are receiving Cream of Asparagus Soup instead. Cream of Broccoli Soup should be back again for your next visit.' She thanked me for my answer. If I did not know any better, I would think we were running a Ritz Carlton Hotel!

*Note: This recipe is close to what we served in jail except we used reconstituted non fat dry milk powder (lower fat content and better for them) and frozen broccoli florets instead of fresh. (Of course the dollop of sour cream was never an option) I have to say that the recipe below is very close to the jail recipe in taste. It is so good even your kids will love it!

- 1 stick, (4 ounces) margarine
- ½ cup chopped onions
- ½ cup all purpose flour
- 4 cups chicken broth
- 2 pounds (4 cups) fresh broccoli florets
- ½ teaspoon white pepper (not black pepper as inmates do not trust little black things in a white soup)
- ½ teaspoon salt
- 2 cups milk, regular or low fat or half and half
- Sour cream for garnish, optional

1. In a large saucepan, melt the margarine over medium heat.
2. Add the onion and sauté for 1 minute.
3. Add the flour and mix well; cook for 1 minute.
4. Mix in the chicken stock and broccoli; bring to a simmer and cook for 30 minutes.
5. Add the pepper and salt; whisk in the milk or half and half.
6. Heat for 5 minutes. Serve with a dollop of sour cream on the top. (optional)

CARROT CAKE (Serves 8-10)

When we served carrot cake to the inmates, we made this cake on a sheet pan and cut it into squares. Since we had a limited budget, we frosted it with our butter cream frosting instead of cream cheese frosting and omitted the raisins and nuts unless we received them through a government commodity program for almost nothing. It was still one of their favorites and delicious!

Senior Cook "Mac" Mac Donald, who worked in the East Mesa Detention Facility, would hold a baking class for those kitchen inmate workers who wanted to learn. He would make an almost exact version of this carrot cake with them; they loved it! Mac is a good example of the many talented cooks we have in Corrections; always going the extra mile.

When I worked for Francis Parker School the main cook, Ms Josie Cruz, had a fabulous Carrot Cake recipe. She made one with only nuts, one with only raisins and one plain so that children who were allergic (or fussy) could have the cake. I brought that recipe with me to the jail to use as our base recipe and the rest is history. Thanks, Josie, from me and a couple of million inmates and staff.

- 2 cups all purpose flour
- 2 ¼ teaspoons baking soda
- 1 ½ teaspoons baking powder
- 3 teaspoons cinnamon
- ¾ teaspoon salt
- 1 ½ cups sugar
- 1 cup vegetable oil
- 4 large eggs
- 3 cups finely grated carrots
- ¾ cup crushed pineapple, drained
- 1 ½ cups walnuts, chopped
- 1 ½ cups golden raisins

1. Preheat oven to 350 degrees
2. Whisk together in a large bowl the flour, baking soda, baking powder, cinnamon and salt.

3. In another large bowl, whisk together until smooth the sugar, oil and eggs.

4. Stir the flour mixture into the egg mixture just until combined.

5. Stir in carrots, pineapple, walnuts and raisins, just until incorporated.

6. Pour batter into a greased 9x12x2 inch pan or Bundt pan.

7. Bake at 350 degrees for 30-35 minutes until done or until a toothpick inserted into the middle of the cake comes out with a few moist crumbs on it.

8. Cool and frost with lemon cream cheese frosting or frosting of your choice; keep refrigerated.

Chapter 1
Before God Made Man

Man plans, God laughs.
(Old Yiddish saying)

In the beginning, before God made man (maybe not that far back but almost), I was just a baby, living over Daddy's diner in Elizabeth, New Jersey, right out there on Route 9. Dad had gotten out of the Army after WW ll. He had always dreamed of his own little place where he could cook for others like he liked to do instead of the Army's way.

Dad's brother Ralph, his wife Dolly, and their baby Tony lived there with us as well. We were just one big happy Italian family, laughing and fighting and working hard, except for my Mom. She was from England and a nurse so she was less than thrilled with this arrangement. So.... you guessed it, after a while Dad went back in the Army and stayed there for the next 18 years.

I literally grew up on Army cooks' knees and under their feet at the many Army posts we lived on for years. My Dad worked every holiday and I grew up for a long time thinking that it was normal for our family to eat Christmas dinner in a mess hall with a few hundred soldiers. As a teenager I thought it was lots of fun and did not mind it one bit.

When I was in 5th grade, we moved to Ft. Hamilton in Brooklyn, NY. Now we were near to almost *all* the Italian American family on my father's side. My mother was again overjoyed!

My grandparents had emigrated from Naples, Italy; my daddy was born in Brooklyn, one of 10 children. First his mother and then his father died so he and two of his brothers were put in an orphanage. Eventually his married sister got them out and took them to live with her; he was devoted to my Aunt Mary for that until the day she died. For example, when he came back from the war after being gone for three years, the first place he went was his sister's house where he promptly fell asleep. When Aunt Mary called my mother to tell her that he was back, it was yet again a joyful thing for her. I am surprised she didn't kill him. I think she would have if she was Italian.

My family was involved in a string of bars and restaurants throughout Brooklyn and also connected in various degrees to the "Family". I thought nothing of seeing some of my uncles and cousins with guns under their jackets. I was told if I ever was in trouble all I had to do was make a call. Thank goodness I never had to do it. Of course this did not make my very refined, educated English mother happy either but what could you do; she had fallen for my dad and that was that.

My Dad literally had a third grade education, obtaining a GED equivalent in the Army. He went on to be a great manager, chef and restaurant owner. He was wonderful with people, particularly those of different races and economic levels, and they adored him. No matter what job he had, everyone worked their best for him and that made him successful, not only in business, but in life. I really learned from the best of the best.

My Dad did not cut me any slack when I worked for him; if someone called in sick I was expected to work a second shift doing that job without complaint. (Not out loud, anyway) However, no one was allowed to even look like they were going to hurt me.

For example, I was working as a waitress at the Holiday House Restaurant on the New Jersey Garden State Parkway. My Dad managed all of them at that time. A group of people came in from Atlantic City and they were all pretty high. That was OK until one guy got really out of hand and fondled my bottom.

I got so upset that I dropped a full tray of cold drinks in his lap. He started screaming at me and wanted to see the manager. So I said, "Daddy, this guy was touching me and wants to see you". I thought the guy was going to pass out right there as my Dad came over to the table with blood in his eyes. He literally ran out of there with my Dad right behind him; it is great to be loved.

I not only learned the restaurant business from the ground up working for my Dad in various places but I also learned what I did not want to do. Among these things was to be a cook, dishwasher or waitress. Even though I could do these jobs well, I particularly loved the management part of the business, working with all the different disciplines within the industry to create and make things happen.

I went to college and I was an English major, aspiring to be a college professor. It never happened. What did happen was marriage to a career Navy guy and children. We moved at least every two years and when I looked for a job, I invariably wound up in food services.

I tried to sell cemetery property once but even though I was giving away one cemetery plot and selling the other one, I couldn't make it work. With my personality I couldn't get people to believe they may die some day and maybe soon.

I tried managing a string of stationary stores but left before the training was over. Do you know how many different types of pencils there are not to mention envelopes? Who cares, right? I was bored before I started.

Therefore, I worked in various types of foodservices, all of which prepared me for going to jail. I was both a public and private school food service manager. I ran large restaurants, including bars and lounges and a disco (that was fun) and two Elk Lodges. I was a manager for two hospitals and two different hotels, both large and small. I was even a food critic for a small newspaper which I enjoyed.

I was foolish enough to go into the restaurant business with my father and my husband. It was called Gregory's, after our son, and it ate up literally every waking minute. Working with various uncles and cousins was no picnic; everyone thought *they* were in charge during the few hours they chose to work. Most of the time it was like an Italian comedy!

For instance, one night the air conditioning went out so my two uncles went out to investigate. One of them held the ladder and the other one went on the roof; coming down didn't go so well. He fell on top of his brother. We had a packed house and these two ran through the middle of the dining room, one carrying a hammer, yelling in Italian at the top of their lungs and then ran back through and out the door.

Everyone had stopped eating and you could hear a pin drop. I stared clapping and said that was part of the show so everyone clapped and continued to eat. It was the hardest job I ever had; when it caught fire one day and we closed it, I could have wept for joy.

There was only one other job I hated more and that was the pig butchering plant in Smithfield, Virginia. One of my friends was a manager for a foodservice contractor and they had just picked up the contract for foodservices for over 3000 factory workers. She needed someone to work there for 3 months to set up the new operation and get it running smoothly.

It sounded like fun until I got out of my car on the first day on the job. The smell is something I shall never forget; it is hard to describe which is lucky for you. The next day was even worse; that was the day they were burning the hair off the pig skin. I never got the smell out of some of my clothes. It was the longest three months of my life.

We cleared out the old equipment from the kitchen, disturbing a large amount of creeping and four legged things. I was taking inventory in the storeroom and was eating my lunch as I worked. Out of the corner of my eye, I saw something moving. A bunch of roaches were trying to drag my chicken leg away and doing a good job of it. That was the last time I ate there until the place was totally fumigated!

We did manage to clean it up and start a new, improved meal service for them. We fed them in groups of 300 people from a cafeteria line. The first group came through and we had made veal parmesan; they didn't know what it was so....... they didn't eat it; they just ate more chicken. For the next three hundred people who came through, we put chicken gravy on top of the veal and they ate it. I learned to keep it simple from then on.

The 600 people who worked the "killing floor" came in to eat in their bloody white coats. (Why they gave them *white* coats I will never know). I went to see the management and told them that I couldn't feed bloody people in my dining room because it was against the law, (I left out the fact that it was "my" law), so they made them change their coats after that.

When the killing floor was operating there was almost no water pressure so my soda machines went down. I put a sign on the area that said "out of order"; the people still tried to make it work. So I put a sign out that said "Broke". That didn't work either; who knew that most of them couldn't read? I had to tape up the machine until I figured out the problem and got the management to not use the water until feeding time was over.

The minute the three months were up and the customer signed their contract for the next 5 years, I was out of there. I have avoided eating ham ever since; it brings back too many memories.

Each job I had helped to prepare me for the jails. Managing large places where my staff and I were the only *sober* people prepared me for dealing with a bunch of inmates who were impaired after many years of indulging in liquor and drugs. The school jobs gave me experience in feeding children and participating in the school lunch program, all of which I did for the Juvenile Facilities. Since male inmates eat a lot like kids, I was *doubly* prepared.

Managing hospital food services was very helpful for me as we had hundreds of inmates who were medically challenged and who were on all sorts of diets. We had diabetic diets, heart diets, Aids patients, dialysis patients, allergies and everything in between.

As the jails are like large hotels with iron bars, my experience working with hotels assisted me as well. For example, I learned that operating your own hotel laundry was very cost productive. I ended up recommending a central laundry and assisting in its' design for the Sheriff.

The "smells "of the butchering plant got me ready for all the distinct smells of the jails that were never as bad. In every job I had I was encouraged to think "outside the box" to improve the program; this made my work much more involved but also rewarding and fun.

I also did some consulting work for various establishments before going to jail. This helped me immensely as one of the first things I did for the Sheriff was a study of the foodservices program.

I recommended that if we were to have good, consistent food that met all regulations, was safe to eat and legally defendable, we needed to centralize our services. We needed to get the cooking out of the hands of the inmates. I realized that I could not continue to be responsible for the status quo. I had created a huge challenge for myself. Thanks to my training and to the many different positions I had during my career, I was ready and willing to do it.

FAMILY RECIPES

I used many of my own recipes as a basis for the recipes I used for the San Diego Jailhouse menu. Here are some of those recipes; I hope you enjoy them as much as my family has over the years.

EASY ENGLISH PIE CRUST (Serves 6-8)

I received this pie crust recipe from my mom and she got it from *her* English mother. It is quick and easy and requires no rolling out. It has a sweet, crumbly taste which is delicious with any kind of filling. I used it in school menus as well as for jail inmates and staff. We just made a large amount of crust and put it on 18x26 sheet pans. We cut the pie into 54 squares before serving. When you are feeding a couple of thousand people it is way easier to do it this way instead of individual pies.

In the case of serving it in jails, it also made the pie harder to steal. We made round pies only for the staff but always made extra ones as they seemed to have magical wings.

- 1 ½ cups flour
- 1 teaspoon salt
- 3 tablespoons sugar
- ½ cup vegetable oil
- 3 tablespoons milk

1. Preheat oven to 375 degrees
2. Place the flour in a pie pan.
3. Sprinkle the salt and sugar over the flour; mix with a fork. Make a well in the middle of the flour.
4. Pour the ½ cup oil into a 1 cup measuring cup. Add the milk to the oil and mix well with a fork.
5. Pour the oil and milk mixture into the well in the pie pan.
6. Quickly mix the flour and oil mixture together with a fork.
7. With your hands, spread the dough out evenly in the pie pan and up the sides. Crimp the edges with a fork. Prick the bottom of the crust a few times with a fork.
8. If you are filling the crust with a pudding or cream mixture that does not need to be baked, bake the crust first at 375 degrees for about 15 minutes or until light brown. Cool the crust before adding the filling.
9. To make a pie where the filling needs to be baked, such as apple or other fruit, place the filling into the raw crust in the pie pan and then bake in a 350 degree oven for approximately 65 minutes or until done. I always make pumpkin pies for

Thanksgiving with this crust. Put the pumpkin filling in the raw crust. Bake at 425 degrees for 15 minutes and then at 350 degrees for 35-40 minutes.

10. You can make another crust to crumble on top of the pie or make a streusel crumb topping and add before baking the pie.

CHEESECAKE ALA RUSSO (Serves 8-10)

As far as I know, this cheesecake recipe has been made by the Italian side of our family for at least 60 years. For the past 20 years or so, my cousin, Tony Russo, has made this cake for special family occasions. Even though there are some of us that can make it, we leave it to Tony as he does it so well. (That should teach him) This is a true *New York* Cheesecake as it doesn't have that graham cracker crust. It forms its' own pie-like crust as it bakes.

When we moved to San Diego from the East Coast we really missed some of the food that they only seem to have or make correctly back home. Cheesecake is one of these items. We finally found one restaurant in San Diego who had it flown in from a bakery in NY and of course it was expensive. So....now we wait for Tony to make it for us.

- 4 large eggs
- I pint ricotta cheese or cottage cheese
- 16 ounces cream cheese, softened
- I pint sour cream
- 3 tablespoons flour
- 3 tablespoons cornstarch
- I tablespoon vanilla
- I ½ cups sugar

- ¼ (1 stick) pound margarine, melted
- ½ cup candied fruit, optional

1. Preheat oven to 325 degrees
2. Using a food processor with a steal blade, or a blender, cream the eggs and ricotta or cottage cheese together until creamy. (I really prefer ricotta cheese)
3. Add the cream cheese and mix well.
4. Add all other ingredients, one at a time and mix until blended.
5. Grease a 10" spring form pan with margarine and fill with mixture. Note: if the pan is non-stick, do not grease the pan.
6. Bake in a 325 degree oven for approximately one hour or until the cake pulls away slightly from the sides and is lightly browned.
7. Turn the oven off and leave the cake in the oven for one hour.
8. Chill uncovered over night and then cover it. Keep it refrigerated until serving.
9. You can top this cake with canned cherry or blueberry pie filling or with fresh fruit such as strawberries.

*Note: I used my blender for the first 2 steps and then transferred the mixture to my mixer. My blender is not big enough to handle all the ingredients so you may have the same problem.

DAD'S PORK AND TOMATO GRAVY (Serves 8)

My Dad's family was from Naples, Italy, and he was an Italian Chef. I used his tomato gravy recipe, without the pork, as the basis for the one we made for the inmates. We sometimes substituted ground beef or ground turkey or a mixture of both.

Dad did everything from scratch and ignored modern conveniences like a micro wave or pressure cooker. Unlike my Dad, I use a pressure cooker which is a lot faster. If you are using one, here are the directions:

In step 4 put the lid on the pressure cooker and set the heat to medium. When the steam starts coming out of the hole, put the little top on. When the top starts to shake, reduce the heat, maintaining the soft shaking. Cook for 45 minutes. Turn off the heat and let it sit for 15 minutes. Carefully remove the top and lid; stir and check to make sure the meat is falling apart.

No matter what method you use, the cook should always test the sauce by dipping several pieces of Italian bread into the gravy and tasting it. This is *absolutely* necessary to make it authentically Italian. This is why the mother or grandmother is never seen to be eating while sitting down. We do all our "small tastes" standing up. So who could eat after that already?

- 2 tablespoons olive oil
- 3-4 pounds pork shoulder
- 4 cloves garlic, minced
- I large can (28 ounces) tomato sauce
- I large can (28 ounces) crushed tomatoes
- I large can, (28 ounces) diced tomatoes
- I tablespoon garlic salt
- I tablespoon garlic powder
- I tablespoon sugar
- I tablespoon black pepper
- I tablespoon dried basil
- I tablespoon oregano

1. In a large pot, over medium heat, brown the pork on both sides in the olive oil; remove the pork and set aside.

2. Add the garlic to the oil and lightly brown.
3. Add all the remaining ingredients; stir well.
4. Place the pork in the sauce; bring to a simmer.
5. Partially cover and simmer for at least two-three hours or until the pork is tender and breaks into pieces.
6. Note that the sauce will be thick, hence the name "gravy".

AUNT DOLLY'S CRUMB CAKE (Serves 6)

This is a simple but delicious coffee cake that was made all over New York by my various relatives but our Aunt Dolly made it the best. She likes to double the topping recipe which makes for a really delicious sweet cake. (You can too if you want to)

Aunt Dolly was always our most favorite Aunt. She is pure Italian but does not look it; 4 foot something with bright red hair, very fair skin and light blue eyes. She is fun and crazy and we love her and her cake! I used the basics of her recipe to make crumb cake for the inmates for breakfast; they loved it too.

Crumb Topping:
- 1 stick (4 ounces) cold butter, cubed
- 1 cup all purpose flour
- 3 teaspoons cinnamon
- 6 tablespoons sugar

Cake:
- 1/2 stick (2 ounces) butter
- ½ cup granulated sugar
- 1 large egg
- 1 ¼ cups all purpose flour

- 1 ½ teaspoons baking powder
- ½ teaspoon salt
- 1 teaspoon vanilla extract
- ¾ cup milk, regular or low fat
- 1 cup powdered sugar

1. Preheat oven to 350 degrees
2. In a small bowl, mix all crumb topping ingredients together with your fingers to form crumbs; set aside.
3. In a mixer on medium speed cream the butter and sugar together; add the egg and mix well.
4. Add all the dry ingredients, except for the powdered sugar, and mix for one minute.
5. Add the vanilla and milk and mix for one minute.
6. Pour into a greased square (8"x8") cake pan. Top with the crumb mixture.
7. Bake at 350 degrees for 30 minutes or until the toothpick comes out with a few moist crumbs on it.
8. Sprinkle the warm cake liberally with powdered sugar and cover with foil or saran wrap.
9. The cake can be served cold or warm.

TONY' SALAMI BREAD (Serves 20)

My cousin, Anthony Russo (Tony), has made this Salami Bread as an appetizer for many of our family functions for years. My daughter, Jessica Battle, started making it when Tony couldn't be there or was making something else. She brings a little of the new generation to the recipe.

She uses Italian (Reduced Fat) 4 Cheeses mixture instead of the mozzarella and she cooks it on a "stone" instead of a sheet pan. No one knew the difference. They both make a few "all cheese" versions, replacing the salami with additional cheese and sprinkling a little cheese on top to mark it as "all cheese". It can be served with or without tomato sauce for dipping.

This started out being for me as I do not like salami and others now like it as well. What is not to like? Bread and melted cheese is always good, with or without a little wine.

- Bridgeford Reddy Dough, 3 each, 1 pound loaves
- 18 slices (6 ounces) hard salami, chopped
- 6 cups shredded mozzarella cheese
- 3 large eggs, beaten with a little water

1. Preheat oven to 375 degrees
2. Defrost the dough and let it sit in a warm place for an hour. *Note: you can make your own bread dough to use here but we have used Bridgeford frozen dough for years because it is easier.
3. Roll each loaf to about ½" thick.
4. Spread 1/3 of the salami and cheese on each loaf.
5. Roll them up, tucking in the sides to seal them.
6. Brush each one with the beaten egg mixture.
7. Bake on an ungreased cookie sheet at 375 degrees for about 20 minutes until golden brown.
8. Cool on a wire rack for about a ½ hour and then slice and serve.

STEVE'S FUDGE CREAM CHEESE FROSTING
(24 cupcakes or one cake)

We used this recipe in San Diego as the basis for our chocolate and mocha frostings; we just didn't use cream cheese due to the cost and calories. Of course I adore this version; it is sinfully rich and easy. I sometimes put some in the freezer to nibble on after meals for that little taste of sweet. With icing like this, who needs cake?

- 8 ounces cream cheese, softened (regular or low fat)
- ¼ pound (one stick) unsalted butter, softened
- 1 teaspoon vanilla
- 4 tablespoons unsweetened cocoa powder
- ½ teaspoon salt
- 3 cups powdered sugar
- 1-2 tablespoons milk (regular or low fat)

1. With an electric mixer on medium speed beat the cream cheese, butter and vanilla until smooth.
2. Add the cocoa powder and salt on low speed until incorporated.
3. Add the powdered sugar in thirds on low speed. Increase to medium speed and beat one minute or until smooth.
4. Add the milk a little at a time until the frosting is the right consistency.

Chapter 2
Going Behind Bars

"Fish and visitors stink in 3 days."
—*Ben Franklin*

My journey to find a cause, create a wonder or save someone from misery and misfortune began on a cool, rainy morning in San Diego on the second day of January, 1986. I was driving down Route 805 on my way to work where I supervised a food service for a large hospital. The meridians dividing the freeways were filled with the soft beauty of bushes of white fluffy flowers. It reminded me of gently blowing drifts of snow, without all the cold, as they swayed in the breeze. I should be happy, yes?

However, I realized I was feeling kind of depressed which is normal for me at the beginning of the New Year. I always go over my resolutions; they were not much different than the previous years; you know, lose weight, exercise more, improve my life and spend more time with family. This year was a little different; I was a lot more depressed than usual. I had not been able to find a job that paid decent money in my profession which didn't involve 80 hours a week, including nights and weekends.

My husband had retired from the Navy after almost 30 years due to poor health and was not able to work so I needed to make a better salary. Therefore, finding this perfect job was at the top of my list. The newspapers were filled with restaurant, hotel or resort jobs. They were not for me anymore. What about the ad for a Chief of Food Services with the Sheriff's Department, I thought for the hundredth time? Every time I read it, I was intrigued. But what was a "Chief", anyway? Would I need to have a degree in Corrections or something?

Providing food for inmates didn't sound all that difficult but it sure didn't sound like much fun. I was looking for a challenging, satisfying job which I could do for the next twenty years. Wow, I could actually have a career now we were settled in one place for a change, I thought. Why not look into the Chief's job and see what happens, I decided.

I can honestly say that I never really thought about jails or prisons, never mind what they ate. I just assumed that it would be gruel, bread and water with lots of beans thrown in for good measure. The only down side I could see was I had always wanted to supply the best quality food and services I possibly could within the confines of the budget.

I applied for the position and a mere eight months later, after being interviewed by several panels and 20 other people, examined inside and out, back ground checked and taking a polygraph, I was offered the job. Before they asked me to accept or not, they gave me a tour of the old downtown Central Jail, probably to see if I would run away. My tour guide was a beautiful and elegantly dressed personnel officer named Ann. She took me out of the administration side of the facility over to the jail itself and I walked into the door I had been so afraid of in the beginning; it all began to get very real.

When you first enter the jail you are let into a sally port. It is like a concrete hallway with doors at both ends, separating the entrance of the building from the jail itself. When the heavy metal door behind you clangs noisily shut, you start thinking you may never get out. I was starting to perspire again and feel claustrophobic. The other door finally rattled its' way open and I felt relief for one second. And then it hit me!

Let me tell you, jails are a lot about smells! It is a combination of a really ripe fish with a very old gym and thousands of unclean bodies. They said that I would get used to it; they lied, I never did. I can still summon up the smell.

After a ride in an old iron elevator that shook a little more with every floor, with chained inmates facing the back wall watching me out of the sides of their eyes, I walked down a long hallway into the kitchen. The smells were a little better; baked beans and hot dogs had just been served for lunch. But I could smell the underlying smells of old grease and water caught beneath the tiles, something akin to carnivals on the day after they close. Over riding this was the smell of unwashed men. (Women in the women's jail have an intoxicating smell all their own)

The inmate kitchen workers were standing around dressed in dirty regular inmate uniforms, most were unshaven and some were smoking. All of them were watching Ann and myself walk through the kitchen. I had been told not to make eye contact with them, no matter what. No problem there. I looked at the kitchen instead and the list of violations grew in my head.

We were escorted by a food service staff member. In contrast to the inmates, he wore a silk shirt, unbuttoned half way down his chest, all the better to see his gold chains. He smelled like cheap cologne which clashed with the various other smells.

The kitchen was dark, with most of the lights off. I assumed they kept it this way so you wouldn't notice the dirt. It was hard to miss it as we walked through ankle high refuse; old potato skins, paper hats and cups and the Lord knows what else. I thought I saw something move and walked faster. This kitchen practically cried out for help.

That day they were feeding 1200 people and I actually felt sorry for them having to eat food that came out of this kitchen. I couldn't wait to leave and I was happy that no one offered me a taste of anything. I would have hated to be rude.

Talk about a *challenge*. Instead of scaring me off I figured "what the hell"; all I could do was *better*. I told the commander who conducted my last interview that day that if he did not want good food, not to hire me. I explained that my strong belief was that inmates are human beings and literally our customers; we should serve good food, even if it was the best gruel in the country.

Seven long weeks went by before I got the call that offered me the job. They said that good food would be a welcome change. That was the start of the best, most challenging, most rewarding, most fun time I have ever had working anywhere. I thoroughly enjoyed myself for the next 21 years.

EASY CHOCOLATE CAKE

This cake was one of the all time favorites with the inmates, juvenile wards and staff. It was an old family recipe from the 1960's and I enlarged it to fit each jail's population. When we started our Central Production Center, I had to enlarge it again to fit the massive mixers. No matter what, it always came out wonderful.

It keeps well and is moist even days later; of course this was never a problem as it disappeared immediately. I had it on the menu with a casserole meal, which was the inmates' least favorite entree, and I never had any complaints. They loved the cake! A little chocolate really goes a long way to make people happy.

Variation: You can add ½ cup of chocolate chips to the batter before baking for extra chocolate taste. I forgot to do this once and when I remembered it was half way through the baking process. So as not to miss the extra chocolate I added them to the top of the cake and continued baking the cake. It came out great!! The chips stayed on the top and were now right under the frosting so you get that extra crunch.

- 1 ¾ cups all purpose flour
- 1 ¼ cups sugar
- 1 ½ teaspoons baking soda
- ¾ teaspoon salt
- ½ cup unsweetened cocoa powder
- 1 ¼ cups milk, regular or low fat
- 2 tablespoons white vinegar
- ¾ cup vegetable oil
- 1 tablespoon vanilla extract

1. Preheat oven to 350 degrees
2. Mix the flour, sugar, baking soda, salt and cocoa powder in a mixing bowl.
3. Add the vinegar to the milk and let stand 5 minutes.
4. Add the milk mixture, oil and vanilla to the flour mixture and beat at medium speed with an electric mixer for approximately two minutes or until smooth.
5. Pour into a greased Bundt pan or 9x12 baking pan. Bake at 350 degrees for 25-30 minutes or until a toothpick inserted into the middle of the cake comes out with a few moist crumbs on it.
6. Frost with Mocha Frosting or a frosting of your choice.

MOCHA FROSTING (Enough for 24 cupcakes or one cake)

- ¼ pound, one stick, unsalted butter, softened
- 4 tablespoons unsweetened cocoa powder
- ½ teaspoon salt
- 3 ½ cups powdered sugar
- 5 tablespoons cold, *very strong* coffee

1. Beat the butter until smooth with an electric mixer.
2. Add the cocoa powder and salt on low speed until incorporated.
3. Add the powdered sugar in thirds on low speed. Increase to medium speed and beat 1-2 minutes until smooth.
4. Add the coffee a little at a time until the frosting is the right, spreadable consistency.
5. Frost the cake and store covered until served.

SWEET AND SOUR SAUCE

You can use this simple, delicious sauce in various ways: for a dipping sauce for food such as fried chicken strips or chicken nuggets, as a sauce for fried cubes or shredded pieces of pork for Sweet and Sour Pork or on any kind of chicken for Sweet and Sour Chicken. We did this in our jails and it was a favorite with our inmates, Juvenile wards, senior citizens and staff alike. No matter what I put this sauce on top of, they would eat it and like it. As they say, the "secret is in the sauce".

- 1/3 cup white vinegar
- 4 tablespoons sugar
- 1 teaspoon soy sauce
- ½ teaspoon ground ginger
- ½ teaspoon garlic powder
- 1 can (8 ounces) crushed pineapple
- ¼ cup green peppers, chopped
- ¼ cup fresh carrots, chopped
- 2 teaspoons cornstarch
- 4 teaspoons cold water

1. Mix together the vinegar, sugar, soy sauce, ginger, garlic powder, pineapple, green peppers and carrots in a medium saucepan.
2. Bring to a boil over medium heat. Simmer for 5 minutes.
3. Add cornstarch to the water to form a paste.
4. Stir the paste into the hot mixture and continue cooking until thickened. (Note: For a little extra zing, use rice vinegar instead of white and increase the sugar to 6 tablespoons. If you want the sauce to be red, add 1 tablespoon of catsup before the cornstarch mixture.) Yield is 2 cups.

Chapter 3
First Day Shock

Be a fearless cook.
Keep your knives sharp and toujours bon appétit.
—Julia Child

My first day on the job was interesting, to say the least. I survived the sally port and the elevator ride to the 7th floor, only to find my desk sitting by the elevator when I got out. It was banged up and splintered; they had retrieved it out of salvage, just for me. I was the first Food Service Chief they ever had and a desk was needed so why not get one from salvage! I tore my stockings for two weeks on the chipped wood before I figured out how to get it *back* to salvage and I found myself a better desk in the basement storage room.

The door to my office was a large, old fashioned metal door with the biggest key hole I had ever seen with a huge key to match. I opened it and the first thing I saw was my secretary; a cute, young blond woman, in old faded jeans with her feet up on her desk, reading a magazine. She proceeded to tell me how unhappy she was to be sent to Central Jail and to Food Service on top of that, just because of a minor infraction. She thought she was being punished.

Within a week we had worked out an agreement. I sent her to my other office in the women's jail which was more to her liking and she dressed professionally and actually started to do secretarial work that I assigned her. She turned out to be a great secretary and really helped me get through my first few years before she left me to get married.

But let us get back to my first day. After a long, hard day trying to get the kitchen staff to talk to me, I was *really* ready to go home. The large metal door to my office was kind of rusted and hard to lock and unlock.

In a jail, you are locked into each space and you lock it when you leave as well. I had let myself out into the kitchen walkway and was trying to lock the door when I saw something out of the corner of my eye; it was a bunch of naked men! I looked again and yes, I was correct; there were at least 20 of them, all bent over no less, and facing the wall. I couldn't get the door unlocked fast enough to get back inside!

I hurriedly went back into my office and locked the door. I tried to figure out why they were there, why they were naked and how in the world I could get to the elevator to go home.

I called downstairs to the Watch Commander. I told the Sergeant that I wanted to leave but there were naked men in my way. He went hysterical and asked if I had ever seen naked men before. I told him that was not the point; Section 2, Page 3, Paragraph 7, of the federal code clearly stated "no nude people in a kitchen". Therefore we were in direct violation of the law. He said, that is a different story and that he would fix it immediately!

I heard him call the deputy in the hallway on the radio. He told him we were in violation of codes and regulations and to get the inmates dressed and out of there immediately. It was a few years before I told him that I made it all up. I just gave him something he could relate to. I have yet to find anything in the food code or a regulation concerning "no nude people" in a kitchen but it just stands to reason, yes? Think of all those burnt parts; soooo not pretty!

I found out the inmates are strip searched in and out of the kitchen to assure that they are not hiding anything in their clothes or on or *in* their bodies. This was all well and good but it was <u>not happening</u> in my kitchens. I put out a memo to all the jails the next day establishing a rule that all strip searching was to be done away from the kitchens.

The second day on the job was even more fun! I had told my Assistant Chief on Friday that the kitchen was filthy and to have the inmates clean it over the weekend. Well, it was Monday and it was even worse. So I told him again what I wanted done. It took me telling his staff *directly* what I expected them to do to get the proper results. It went a lot easier when I explained how much happier they would be working in a clean, well run kitchen and they agreed.

In the meantime, I observed the portioning of the food into trays. The trays were large heavy, insulated plastic trays that normally had white dishes inserted in the holes to put the food into but not in jail; the food just went into the holes. When I asked the Senior Cook in charge why there were no dishes, he sort of grumbled at me that the inmates would break them and cut each other up with the pieces. Good point.

I asked where the napkins were and got a "look" which said that I had to be the dumbest woman walking; didn't I know where I was? The next question I asked was why they did not get at least powdered creamer to go with their coffee. It seems that it is flammable and that the inmates would save it up to use it to make pipe bombs, of all things. The things you learn in jail! Needless to say, I never used powdered creamer in my coffee again.

Now I must stop here and explain about Senior Cook Willie. He was an older man, kind of rough and tough, who wore a perpetual scowl on his face. He grumbled orders out of the side of his mouth at the inmates and always looked extremely unhappy. I didn't improve his mood by observing him and asking stupid questions.

The "piece de resistance" was when he tried to feed 1200 people, 3 ounces of meatloaf each, with only 200 pounds of meat. He had no choice but to do all the trays correctly up to the last meals where he ran out of meat. I asked why he did not prepare enough meat loaf and he told me that the Assistant Chief, who had been the boss up to my coming on board, said that was all he could have because of the budget. The Assistant Chief said that they were "only" inmates and were lucky to get anything to eat.

This guy and I definitely did not have the same set of priorities so within 6 weeks he left me for greener pastures. Along with him went the Food Service staff member in the silk shirt; I heard that he went to work at a State prison where the inmates promptly threw him off the back dock; he retired from Corrections after that happened. Everyone else was happy to stay and from then on we were all one big happy family.

The remaining staff had not had a decent vacation in literally years due to an inadequate number of positions. They had not been given the tools to do the job and team work was not encouraged. No one knew anyone else who worked in any of the other jails. With their help we changed all that.

In the meantime, I made sure that Willie had enough food for each meal and clear directions to follow. I renamed him "Sweet Willie" and tried to get him to smile every day. The name caught on and everyone started to call him Sweet Willie, much to his dismay, from then on. It didn't matter that he told them that wasn't his name; they believed me. I knew he was sweet inside.

I immediately started an Employees Appreciation Program. A year later he really smiled as he accepted the very first "Senior Cook of the Year" award at our first ever Food Service Awards Banquet. These folks *more* than deserved recognition.

In the first few weeks I was there, I had to deal with some interesting problems. First of all, the diabetic inmates went on a hunger strike of all things. I went to see them and found out why they were doing it. It seems the floor inmate workers were taking the "good" things off their trays and messing with their food. I told them I would take care of it and for them to come off their strike and eat. I explained to them it is actually a matter of life and death for them to eat appropriately and take their medicine.

I went to see the Captain and he issued orders to the floor deputies to make sure the trays were not messed with; it didn't always work as there were not enough deputies to assure this would happen. So....I had one of my staff deliver the trays every meal directly to these inmates which fixed the problem.

On another day, the Food Service Supervisor, Mel Valenzuela, called me on the phone because he was being threatened by an inmate with a law suit, of all things. It seems that we had a lawyer in jail for 30 days for getting on the wrong side of a judge. This was his *second* 30 days; I assume that after he was released the first time, he went back to court and did the same thing he did before to the judge; you'd think he would learn!

In our kitchens, the new inmates usually start in the dishwashing area and work their way up. Before he was released, this lawyer had been promoted up to the pantry area preparing salads and he really liked it. Now that he was back in jail, he wanted to *start* in the pantry area and was threatening to sue Mel if he wasn't allowed to do it. I asked Mel to get the inmate and put him on the phone.

I told the inmate about our system but he was having none of it. He told me that I was the Chief and he knew that I could do anything I wanted to do which was really new to me. However, I agreed I could make this particular request happen but I wanted him to consider one thing—his safety. He asked me what I meant and I told him what the other inmates might do to inmates who are shown favors. However, it was his choice; after all he had to sleep sometime. He meekly went back to the scullery. I asked him to stop doing whatever he was doing to the judge as we did not want to see him again. I think this guy would have made a better pantry man than a lawyer.

When two of my ovens went down, I called for a repair man. He was supposed to be there by 11:00am and here it was 2:00pm and he still wasn't there. His company swore he called them from in front of the jail at 10:45am. Since people sometimes are so stupid they do not think the jail will run a check on their license, I figured this guy must be one of them. Sure enough, when I went downstairs, there he was, already booked and waiting to go up to a floor.

I talked to the deputies and explained I needed him to fix my ovens so they sent him to the kitchen along with his tools. I told him to get to work. He said, "Will I get paid?" I asked him just how dumb *was* it to come in a jail with warrants out for his arrest? He said he guessed he deserved it and fixed my ovens without another word.

Now that I think about it, it seems that old Central Jail had its' share of unusual inmates. There was the inmate that I did a dietary consult on that stood on his head the entire time I talked to him. He said that was the only way he could think. He wanted some weird things like no chicken because he was a Christian. I told him I was a Christian as well and this was a new one on me. He spouted off lines supposedly from the Bible and when we got right down to it, he liked the chicken his *mother* used to make. I told him the female cook we had in the kitchen made great mothers' chicken so he agreed to eat it and not make a fuss.

What he really wanted was a spoonful of peanut butter to take with his psychiatric meds like he had done at home. (You guessed it; he was still with mom and yes, this guy was over 40) Since I could see that he definitely needed those meds, he got his peanut butter! Up to this time, he wrote 10 complaints a day but I never heard a word from him again.

The very first inmate that I did a diet consult on was a 65 year old, grandfatherly looking man, chained to a bench, attached to a wall. He had problems with his digestive tract, among other things, so I put him on a gastric soft diet. I was still trying to get over the shock of having to talk in a normal way to a chained man and feeling sorry for him when I decided to look up his info to see how long he would be with us. It seemed he was in for 150 counts of child molestation, under the age of three, with a foreign object! He would be on his way to prison soon for a long time and no, I was no longer sorry for him.

That was only one jail; I had seven more jails to go. I was just starting to have fun!

MISS MARIE'S FRIED CHICKEN

This chicken is "to die for" either eaten hot right away or cold the next day. It doesn't matter what you serve with it; no one would remember it anyway, just the *chicken*.

Ms Marie Chandler was a Sheriff's Senior Cook in our department who was with us almost 20 years. She was called Ms Marie by inmates and staff alike and well respected by all. She worked for the last part of her career at the new Central Jail downtown. When fried chicken was on the menu for the staff, we fed *three times* the number of people than we usually did. They came from other jails, from the Sheriff's Office and the maintenance shops. Thank God there was an iron gate on the front door; we would never have had enough chicken!

The inmates volunteered to work in her area and on her shift to learn from her. She was tough with them but they liked it. And of course, they got to eat her fried chicken. She was known to remind Sheriff Kolender himself of his diet when he came through for lunch and he liked her for that too! (He also got to eat her chicken) She never shared her recipe with anyone but when she retired, she gave us her recipe. Thank you Marie for avoiding a riot!

- 3 pounds chicken parts or skinless thighs and breasts
- I cup flour
- Seasoning Mix:
- I teaspoon salt
- I teaspoon black pepper
- I teaspoon cayenne pepper
- I teaspoon curry powder
- 2 ½ teaspoons garlic powder

- 1 teaspoon cumin
- 2 teaspoons paprika
- ¼ teaspoon all spice
- Vegetable oil for frying

1. Wash the chicken in cold water.
2. Mix all spices together with your fingers until it feels like salt to make seasoning mix.
3. Rub the seasoning mix all over the chicken and let it sit in the refrigerator for a few hours.
4. Dredge the chicken in the flour; shake off the excess flour.
5. Heat enough oil to cover the chicken in a fryer or deep pan.
6. Fry until golden brown and cooked through.

ZUCCHINI BREAD (Yield 2 loaves)

This is moist, dense bread that is great the way it is but you can also add 1 cup of raisins or nuts or both in Step 4 to this recipe. As we ran on a tight budget, we usually did not have these items to add to it. You will find zucchini bread, banana bread or applesauce spice bread in many jails and prisons. It is a great way to use leftover vegetables and the inmates love it. It can be used for breakfast or as a dessert. This is one of the recipes I made over and over for this book and never ran out of eager testers for it. Try this bread for breakfast with a *smear* of cream cheese and fresh fruit on the side; everybody will love it!

- 3 cups flour
- 1 teaspoon salt
- 1 teaspoon baking soda
- 1 teaspoon baking powder

- 3 teaspoons cinnamon
- 3 eggs
- 3 teaspoons vanilla extract
- ½ cup applesauce
- ½ cup vegetable oil
- 1 cup brown sugar
- 1 cup white sugar
- 4 cups grated zucchini

1. Preheat oven to 325 degrees
2. In a large bowl sift together flour, salt, baking soda, baking powder and cinnamon.
3. In another bowl beat eggs, vanilla, applesauce, oil, brown sugar and white sugar together, about 2 minutes.
4. Add the flour mixture to the egg mixture and beat for 2 minutes.
5. Stir in zucchini.
6. Pour into 2 greased loaf pans.
7. Bake in a 325 degree oven for 40-50 minutes or until a tester inserted in the middle of the loaf comes out with a few moist crumbs on it.

RANGER COOKIES (Makes 3 dozen, 3" cookies)

Policemen may like their donuts but inmates and deputies alike *love* their "jailhouse cookies". These cookies were like magic for me. We made them for the inmates, staff, seniors and juveniles who all loved them. In fact, one inmate loved our cookies so much that when she got out, she wrote back for the recipe and enclosed a self addressed stamped envelope; of course we complied.

We had to hide them from the staff or we would run out. No one really knew or cared that they are high fiber cookies. But what I really liked about them is that I would bring them to meetings with me for refreshments and used them to get what I wanted. It worked like a charm. Believe me, the Army is not the only one that travels on their stomach. People seemed to melt when eating these cookies.

- 1 ¾ cups all purpose flour
- ¾ teaspoon baking powder
- ¾ teaspoon baking soda
- ½ teaspoon salt
- ½ teaspoon cinnamon
- 2 sticks, (8 ounces) softened margarine
- 1 ½ cups light brown sugar
- ¼ cup granulated sugar
- 2 large eggs
- 2 teaspoons vanilla extract
- ½ teaspoon maple extract
- ½ cup raisins
- ½ cup chocolate chips
- 3 ½ cups old fashioned rolled oats

1. Preheat oven to 350 degrees. Grease cookie sheets.
2. In a bowl, mix together the flour, baking powder, baking soda, salt and cinnamon.
3. In a separate bowl, beat the butter, brown sugar, white sugar, eggs, vanilla and maple extract on medium speed until well blended.
4. Add the wet mixture to the flour mixture and mix just to incorporate.
5. Stir in the raisins, chocolate chips and oats.
6. Drop the dough by heaping measuring tablespoons onto the cookie sheet, 3" apart.

7. Lightly press the dough down with your fingers to form ½" thick rounds.

8. Bake 1 sheet pan at a time until lightly browned all over and almost firm in the center, 6-9 minutes.

9. Let stand 2 minutes and then remove to a rack to cool.

Note: I also made these cookies when I ran school foodservices, only we called them "Cowboy Cookies". I changed the name to Ranger Cookies when I brought them to the jails. In the school, when the football team won a game, we sent over a box of "just out of the oven" cookies. Needless to say, we won a lot in those years!

Chapter 4
Now for the Second Week

Once a girl has tasted a sugar stick,
she cannot live without suck.
(An old 17th century saying)

I had been given a second office in Las Colinas, the women's jail in Santee. Since the County of San Diego is 2,000 square miles, having an office near the Eastern part of the County came in handy. Also, remember my secretary really wanted out of old Central Jail and she was happier there. The start of my first day at this office is still being talked and laughed about 25 years later. (I am glad I can provide people with amusement)

I arrived at work about 6:00am and as I started to walk from the parking lot to the front door, I noticed a lot of women milling around in front of the building. They were mostly dressed in costumes; it looked like an early trick or treat. There were little school girl uniforms, cheer leaders, angels, bunnies and dance hall girls.

I then noticed these guys in the parking lot waiting for the girls to come to them. They were dressed in fancy shiny suits and fedora hats (some complete with feathers) and were leaning on an assortment of long, fancy cars. I sure got the once over as I walked through everyone and into the lobby.

As I was let into the sally port, I asked the information clerk if they were shooting a movie or something out there. They were all rolling with laughter behind the thick, bullet proof glass window. I didn't understand what was so funny until one of them told me that they were releasing some of the prostitutes that were caught in a sweep the night before. The guys in the parking lot were actually their pimps! I was stuck in the sally port while they told everyone on duty what the "newbie" said. I have yet to live it down! So who knew?

I also learned where they put the "Johns" they picked up at the same time; I had no idea they even did that. They were kept for a few days in Central jail where they had to call their wives to let them know why they were not home and that their cars were impounded. It was kind of interesting to go look at them in their cells, sitting cheek to jowl with the drunks and thieves.

Out of a population of 5,800 inmates, only 1,000 were women. I believe that either we women are not as criminally inclined as men are or we are too smart to get caught.

The lower level, non-violent inmates are selected to be trustee inmate workers. A few years after I started working there, we became so overcrowded that most or all of the inmates we incarcerated were charged with felony crimes and the quality of the inmate worker pool went down.

The workers wore tan uniforms, with the exception of the kitchen workers who wore white; most of the rest of the inmates wore blue. They had more privileges than the main line inmates; most behaved themselves so they wouldn't get put back in mainline which we called "rolling up to blues".

One of the biggest things I had to learn was there is a sub-culture which exists in jails. I remember walking through an intake area where the deputy was spraying the bugs which just came off the new inmates; it sure opened my eyes. Not counting the people who get caught drunk driving or fighting in public once or twice, the vast majority come in and out of jail like it is a motel. They commit crimes over and over and continue to live this way no matter how much we try to rehabilitate them.

Drugs play a major role as 70% of the people coming into jails are involved with drugs or alcohol. When I used to watch prison shows on

TV I thought they made most of it up; not true. I really got educated in the art of dealing with inmates, particularly in our women's jail.

When you entered the women's jail, there was the usual sally port to go through and immediately in front of you was the "fish tank". This was a glassed in cell where we put the new "fish" just coming in to the jail. You could always tell the women who had never been in jail from the prostitutes that treated the experience like "old home week". If you looked to the right you could see some women getting their mug shots and fingerprints done. Many were the times that I thought to myself, "There but for the grace of God go I".

I then walked down a long hallway past the high security cells where some of the inmates were being very noisy in not such a lady like way. Next to them was the waiting area where the inmates sat chained to benches waiting to see the doctor at sick call. It took me a while to get used to seeing people in chains. I had to pass through a large security door to go outside and the grounds reminded me of a school campus with various one story buildings scattered among flower gardens and even a swimming pool in the corner. (Eventually budget constraints closed the pool.) You remembered it was a jail when you saw the high security fences topped with barbed wire all around the area and of course cameras were everywhere.

Except for the bars on the windows and the occasional line of female inmates in uniform being marched to another building, some of them in leg, waist and wrist chains, you would think it idyllic. A gardening inmate crew grew beautiful flowers and trees; it was one of the most popular inmate educational programs. Every day while walking through the grounds to my office, smelling the flowers and enjoying the changing seasons, I could *almost* forget where I was and the abject misery of some of the inmates as well as the blatant evil of their crimes.

When one of our information clerks was killed by her husband with a baseball bat, the inmate workers created a rose garden in her memory that was really beautiful. It was kind of ironic that criminals built a garden for someone because another criminal murdered her. It had quite an impact on everyone at the facility, including the inmates.

Inmate workers were allowed to move from one building to another without an escort. They had to walk on the right side of the walk and when an officer or civilian approached them, they had to stop and face away until the person passed them. They were never allowed to walk directly behind you. Anytime I walked with an inmate, she walked in front of me where I could see her. It took me a while to get used to this but I eventually realized that everything had a good reason; our safety came first.

The women's jail was so different than all the other jails. For one thing, information got around in a nana second. They listened and observed what was going on all the time and passed it down the line. They even got the information to the men they knew in jail in other facilities. If we served something different <u>anywhere</u> everybody knew it and it was commented on and complained about.

Women eat differently than men, as if you men didn't know. By law, inmates must have at least 15 minutes to eat their meal. Since a lot of disturbances happen during meal time, we do not want them all together for very long. Men were done in 10 minutes, tops. They were given only a disposable spoon to eat with and no napkins; they never missed them. They didn't talk much and just wolfed down their food.

Women on the other hand took a lot longer to eat. They examined their food and of course eating a meal was a social occasion. The deputies tried to keep the talking at least to low levels. They also were the only inmates who wanted napkins so we gave them to them.

According to nutritional regulations, the women should have received fewer calories than the men. I didn't bother with that and gave everyone the same meal for two reasons. First of all, the hot line would inform everyone that the men got something more than the women and the complaints would be endless. The second reason was that I could not think of a more stressful situation than being in jail and what do you want to do when under stress? Eat! Why add fat to the fire, so to speak?

We had a fairly nice but old kitchen at this facility where we provided work and training for approximately 30 women inmate workers. We had about 12 on a shift; some of them worked in the staff dining room while others washed dishes and still others prepped the food and did light grill work.

The inmates were dressed all in white uniforms with white hair nets. Except for the San Diego Jail printed across the back, you would think you were in a sparkling clean, well run kitchen in a regular restaurant. In fact, our kitchens were *cleaner* than most restaurants.

Since women inmates are harder to manage than male inmates, we handpicked the Senior Cooks and Supervisor to work with them. The female inmates were sweet to our faces but very devious and clever behind our backs. You had to be on your toes when working with them. In contrast, the male inmates were right in your face and you knew where they were coming from at least, making them easier to handle.

Since a well run food service generates team work and camaraderie we had more of a problem with the staff being too *nice* and too *close* to the inmates rather than abusing them. The inmates would try to get the staff to break the rules by asking them to take notes and letters for them out of the facility or into the facility or by putting money on their books so they could buy things from the Commissary.

Of course they came on to us as well, both men and women. You have to remember that over half of the inmates were prostitutes on the outside and they knew how to work it. Therefore, working there was not an easy job. Sometimes an inmate would get mad at a Sr. Cook and accuse him of doing all kinds of things to her, usually in the freezer. (I would like to see guys capable of doing what they said they did in a *Freezer*) They picked the freezer because they did not think that there were security cameras in there. There had to be an Internal Affairs investigation for all accusations that normally ended with either the inmate or one of her fellow inmates saying they made it up. Such fun!

I did have one 45 year old Senior Cook fall "in love" with a 21 year old inmate worker, a high class call girl, who already had a long rap sheet and three aliases. Of course the other girls ratted on them and we caught him in court with her holding hands.

I talked with him but to no avail. He quit his job, left his pregnant wife and moved in with the inmate after he bailed her out. She wiped him out in two months, leaving him as soon as he was out of money and therefore useless to her. He went back to his wife and I helped him get another job somewhere else. As they say, "there is no fool like an old fool" and he wasn't even that old.

You would not believe what the inmates are capable of doing! I came into the kitchen office one day and my Food Service Supervisor and Senior Cooks were laughing up a storm. I asked them what was so funny and they pointed outside to the kitchen yard. There were two deputies out there and they were measuring the small openings in the chain link fencing that surrounded our backyard and taking notes.

I still didn't see what so funny until they told me the background story. It seems that one of our kitchen inmate workers, who had been with us for 6 months, was now 3 months <u>pregnant</u>. Of course there was an investigation as to how she *got* pregnant and she swore it was her boyfriend. They didn't believe her at first but when they questioned the boyfriend he told them how it happened.

It seems that when it was starting to get dark after dinner, the inmate would meet him by the fence where things evidently got hot and heavy. (That had to hurt) The deputies were measuring the holes in the fence to see if it was possible. I ended up rolling with laughter with my staff. You have to have humor while working behind bars; it sure makes things more tolerable.

A few months later we had one of our inmates escape from the kitchen. It seems that this inmate convinced the night cook that none of the other inmates liked her; she wanted to sit outside by the fence and eat her dinner by herself. So.....he let her. (What; is this High School?) It seems that she worked for a while at the bolts that held the fence onto the gate, maybe with a tool thrown over the fence to her, until she got it loose and part of the fence came loose from the gate.

One night, when she failed to come back in, they went to look for her. The only thing left of her was a pile of white inmate clothes in the backyard. It seems she slathered herself with shortening and slipped through the hole in the fence. As the cook said, "she was only a little bitty thing". Kind of clever too, wouldn't you say? In the end, she wasn't that smart since the first place she went was home where we caught her and brought her back. *She* now had a two year prison term tacked onto her 4 months sentence for escaping jail and *we* got a *double* fence and sally port at the back gate.

Six months later another inmate worker managed to get away. A staff member took a group of low security inmates out to dump the trash and one hid and stayed behind. We knew she was gone in 5 minutes and went immediately into lock down. These lock downs were a royal pain as everything stopped in the jail and no one could leave until it was lifted. We often spent many hours going through the trash, searching for something that was missing, sometimes as small as a fork.

All the inmates had to be counted in their housing units so all work stopped, including the kitchen that was preparing the meals; like I said, a pain. Meanwhile, the inmate who got away turned her shirt inside out so you couldn't see the San Diego Jail printed on it. She walked up the street and started hitchhiking.

A Sheriff's unit pulled over and gave her a lecture on why she shouldn't hitchhike and left! (No one knew she was actually missing yet) It took us a few days to get her back into custody. The deputy got teased for quite a while for not recognizing an escaped inmate. To be fair to the Deputy, they hadn't put out the alarm yet, but still!

A word to the wise, ladies; most of our female inmates will tell you they are in jail because of *men*. It seems to be true as some are there because they chose a guy to live with who brought drugs, guns and worse into the house with their children. These women steal and prostitute for them and neglect and then lose their children as well. Some of them are there because they kill their significant other and according to them, he deserved it.

One of the saddest things I saw was a 60 year old woman who was put in jail for a year because of her husband. Her husband did the tax returns; she never read them, she just signed them. She never worked, had no children and was basically a home body. You guessed it; he lied on his returns. He went to prison for several years. She got a lighter sentence as she was responsible to read what she signed, especially for the government. The inmate workers adopted her as their grandma and protected her. We had her put in the kitchen so we could keep an eye on her as well. She was a nice lady and we were happy for her when she was released.

CATHY'S CORN SALAD (6 servings)

When San Diego Sheriff Senior Cook Cathy Augustine was on duty in the kitchen at the women's jail, the salad bar always looked and tasted extra nice. Over her 18 years with the Sheriff, she trained dozens and dozens of female inmates how to make different salads in the proper way as well as unusual salads out of "this and that". This is one of her recipes which is simple to make and a favorite of everybody there.

- 3 slices bacon
- 2 cans (15 ¼ ounces) whole kernel corn, drained
- ½ medium onion, minced
- ½ red or green bell pepper, chopped
- 1 teaspoon Tabasco sauce
- ½ cup crumbled feta cheese
- ½ cup any Italian dressing

1. Fry the bacon until crisp; drain and crumble it well
2. Mix the bacon with all other ingredients and chill before serving

PRUNE CAKE (HIGH ENERGY CAKE) (Serves 8)

There is an old saying that says that "if you are given lemons, make lemonade". I say "That if you are given prunes, make Prune Cake". The first time I made this cake was when I was a Food Service Director for schools. The Government Commodity Program offered us tons of prunes for almost nothing. Of course prunes are right up there with French fries on a kids' favorite foods list. (Only kidding) So we came up with this delicious cake that we called *High Energy Cake* so the kids would eat it. They loved it and so did the school staff. In fact, the staff ate so much of it that the next day I had a few "tummy" complaints. When I told them it was really *Prune Cake* they understood and used restraint the next time we served it. No one told them to eat six pieces although it is easy to do.

When I went into the jails I found that we were also offered cooked prunes from the Commodity Program. When I started there, they were giving the inmates the prunes for breakfast. You can imagine where they put them and/or threw them. The object of going to the trouble of preparing the meals is to have them actually eat them.

We immediately started to make the High Energy Cake that they grew to love. We iced it with a butter cream frosting due to the higher cost of cream cheese frosting. They still loved it probably because they didn't "know from cream cheese frosting". After a while the government stopped sending us prunes so we switched over to Spice Cake which they liked as well. I actually got requests for the High Energy Cake to come back. We believed in happy inmates. If they only knew....

This is a very dense, fruity and delicious cake that is hard to resist so be careful not to eat too much of it at one time.

Preheat oven to 350 degrees

- 25 ounce jar cooked prunes
- I cup (8 ounces) vegetable shortening
- ¾ cup granulated sugar
- ¾ cup brown sugar
- 3 large eggs
- 2 cups all purpose flour
- I teaspoon baking powder
- I teaspoon salt
- I teaspoon ground cloves
- I teaspoon nutmeg
- 2 teaspoons cinnamon
- I cup reserved prune juice and water

1. If using the cooked prunes in the jar, drain the prunes, reserving the juice. Pit and finely chop the prunes. The yield will be 10 ounces of chopped prunes and 6 ounces of juice. Add 2 ounces of water to the juice to make 8 ounces. Set aside. You can also cook your own prunes as long as you use the same amounts of prunes and juice in the recipe.
2. Cream the shortening in a mixer on medium speed. Add the granulated sugar and brown sugar and mix until creamy.

3. Add the eggs and mix well.
4. Sift the flour together with the baking powder, salt, cloves, nutmeg and cinnamon.
5. Add the flour mixture and the juice to the shortening mixture alternately in two portions. Mix at medium speed for one minute after each addition.
6. Add chopped prunes and mix one minute.
7. Pour mixture into a greased 9x13x2 inch pan.
8. Bake at 350 degrees for approximately 45 minutes until the top is lightly browned and cake springs back when pressed lightly in the center. The cake will be moist.
9. Ice with a cream cheese frosting or icing of your choice. Keep in the refrigerator until eaten.

CRAMIQUE (RAISIN BREAKFAST BREAD) (Serves 8)

Ms Joan Faustman, the Food Service Supervisor at Las Colinas, now retired, submitted this recipe. She made this bread with the kitchen inmates as part of their training and they loved it as much as the inmates in Belgium where it originated.

Making this bread reminded me why I don't usually bake bread. I am not a baker, beyond simple cakes, pies and cookies. I am not precise or patient enough; it makes me appreciate those who are. My first try did not turn out too good but the second one was great. The moral of the story is <u>Pay Attention</u> to the details.

The bread is wonderful; slightly sweet and nice and light. It makes the Best toast; with a little sweet butter and your favorite marmalade, you will think that you have died and gone to heaven. I can see why they serve it for breakfast; those inmates in Belgium are lucky, yes?

Preheat oven to 400 degrees

- 2 cups all purpose flour
- 2 teaspoons active dry yeast
- ½ cup milk, warm
- 2 large eggs
- 4 tablespoons margarine or butter, softened
- 1 teaspoon sugar
- ¾ teaspoon salt
- ¾ cup dark raisins soaked to plump

1. Put 1 ½ cups flour in a mixing bowl.
2. In a small bowl whisk the yeast into the milk and then whisk in the egg yolks.
3. Stir the egg mixture into the flour and mix on the lowest speed for 2 minutes. Let the dough rest for 10 minutes.
4. Add the butter or margarine, sugar, salt and remaining ½ cup flour to the mixture and mix on low speed for 1 minute. Increase to medium speed and mix for 4 minutes longer until the dough is smooth.
5. Mix in the raisins.
6. Put the dough in a buttered bowl, turning the dough over so the top is buttered. Cover with saran wrap and let it rest for one hour in a warm place.
7. After the dough has risen put it on a floured board and shape into a rectangle and then fold in half to fit the pan.
8. Place in a buttered loaf pan. Butter a piece of saran wrap and place it on the dough, buttered side down. Let it rise until double in a warm place for about an hour; remove the saran wrap.
9. Bake at 400 degrees in the middle of the oven for 30 minutes until the bread is a golden color.
10. Remove from the pan and let the bread cool on its side before slicing.

Chapter 5
And Then There Was More

Just as bees make honey from thyme,
the strongest and driest of herbs,
so do the wise profit from the most difficult of experiences.
—Plato

I had eight jails in all when I started with the Sheriff's Department and they were all different. Some were maximum security, some were high rise buildings, one was built below ground and two were medium security "camp like" jails. Each had its' own unique set of rules and needs so it definitely didn't call for an exact cookie cutter Food Service Program. However, the *food* needed to be the same because the inmates traveled between the jails and food is tops on their list. Heaven forbid that they had one thing in one jail and not in another jail; I would hear about it.

The staff was not much better. The food served in the staff dining rooms needed to be the same as well or I would also hear about it. I received an e-mail from one staff member that said that the ranch dressing in one jail was not the same as the one in the jail he was transferred to and could I change it. This guy needed to "get a life" but I was nice about it.

Another one wrote me that they never served spaghetti and meatballs on the days he worked and he wanted me to change the menu. I nicely informed him that spaghetti *actually* existed in other places, like in the grocery store and restaurants. That would have to do until they rotated his schedule in a few months. I also thanked him for the compliment.

The inmate workers who worked in our kitchens ate the same food as we served the staff. The main reason we did this was that if an inmate put something bad in the food *they* would be eating it as well. Other jails that did not properly supervise their workers had incidents of inmates messing with the food for other inmates they didn't like or for the staff and you wouldn't believe the things they did. I will not gross you out by telling you. We made sure that we supervised our workers, treated them fairly and watched them all the time.

We made it a privilege to work in the kitchen so the inmates behaved for the most part. Most of the food came out of the Production Center so the inmates and staff basically had the same menu. The staff food was presented a little differently and we had a short order menu and salad bar for them as well. The staff could eat all they wanted to eat. On occasion, we did serve a few different things like ribs to the staff but not the inmates for obvious reasons. (The bones could be used as weapons) All the inmates got boneless riblets which they loved! Every time McDonald's took the riblets off their menu, we bought the leftover stock at a good price and everyone was happy.

Three of the jails were "booking jails" meaning they took in the people who had been arrested by one of the law enforcement agencies. When you are booked lots of things happen. They try to establish your identity, have a medical staff member evaluate you, take a mug shot and fingerprints and under certain circumstances, do a strip search/cavity search on you. It is the strip search part that keeps me forever on the right side of the law *and* the bars.

They need to establish if you are a he/she or a she/he, or a transvestite; a lot comes down to what "plumbing" you have. In addition, they need to know if you are a gang member and to which gang you belong and if you are a young and tender or old and infirm. They then can house you in the proper cell to await processing or movement to the security floors.

Some people come in so far gone on drugs, they are uncontrollable. They are put into a G cell or isolation for their own protection. These cells have four walls and a hole in the floor to relieve yourself; not very pretty but effective. Sometimes folks lie (Oh really?) and they wind up in the wrong cell to be in for their safety.

One guy said he was a Blood when he really was a Cripps; they had a hell of a time extracting what was left of him out of the cell. Some inmates try to say they are diabetic, thinking we are going to hand them needles which they would keep in case some drugs came their way. When they learn that they will be injected by medical staff they change their minds.

There are two unusual stories I have heard about the booking area that I thought you would like to hear.

In a jail somewhere in the country there were some incidents of the Police Department bringing in prisoners that were unconscious. After they were booked and were resting in the drunk tank for a while, some never woke up due to the fact that they had been <u>dead all along</u>. This proved to be a big problem for the Sheriff. So they passed a rule that the prisoner must walk in on their own to make sure they were alive so …no carry-ins. Makes sense, yes?

One night, the PD did a sweep of the downtown area and brought in a large bunch of "working girls." Two particularly beautiful girls had no priors and were sober and cooperating so they were patted down and put directly into the "fish tank". (This is what we call the holding cell for new inmates or "fish")

About 15 minutes later, the officers heard a lot of noise coming from the tank. The girls were all crowded around something on the floor. When they parted the crowd and looked down, they saw the backsides of two men with girls underneath them. They were horrified that two men had gotten into the tank with the women. When they turned them over, it was the two beautiful girls they had just booked.

The other girls were not happy that the officers broke up the fun and the officers were not happy about the "fun" to begin with. Needless to say, the booking process was modified immediately to check more accurately for "plumbing".

We had a jail in San Diego that they nicknamed "The Styrofoam Jail". It seems that when it was built, the contractor offered to save money for the County by putting what amounted to Styrofoam (They didn't call it that) in between the drywall and the outside wall. Since the inmates do not have much to do but destroy things, someone put his foot through the wall in his cell. When he saw the Styrofoam, he continued digging through to the outside wall and made a hole big enough to fit through.

One night they knotted the sheets together and climbed out the window. The only problem was that they were on the seventh floor and the sheets only reached to the third floor. One lost his grip and fell to the ground and was killed and two were injured. The others just hung there, dangling in the wind, waiting to be rescued.

As I was coming home that night, I went over the top of the hill and I could see the jail in the valley below as it was the tallest building there. It was also lit up by helicopters flying around the jail with their spot lights on it. I could see the sheets hanging down the side of the building and I could hear the deputies on my police radio talking to the inmates hanging from the sheets. The inmates were actually refusing to give them their names; like they had somewhere else to go but up and back through the hole? It was like a scene out of Godzilla, minus the ape.

It didn't stop there. Another group of inmates did the same thing a few weeks later. This time they went out of the building where there were trees and used them to get to the ground. Even though it was late at night the people in a retirement home across from the jail called us and said that there were inmates climbing out of the building. Seven got away that night and it took us a while to get them all back into custody.

I am not done yet. A month later another group tried it again but this time it didn't work. Not only did we have a patrol outside the building to greet them but they had taken the trees away. You should have heard the inmates! They were furious because it seems that the Sheriff played dirty by spoiling their escape. I will tell you one better than that; the family of one of the inmates who was hurt in the fall tried to sue the County for putting their wonderful guy in a jail that "was not safe to break out from". Do you believe it?

Needless to say, we closed the jail and converted it into county offices. I voted to put the female inmates in that jail as women *know* how many sheets it takes to reach the ground safely and therefore wouldn't attempt to break out but I was out voted.

This job always could be relied upon to give me challenges and surprises. About a year or so after I started with the Sheriff, my boss called me in and presented me with a small problem. It seemed that we were closing one of our large maximum security jails for renovation but we still had about 150-200 inmates going there for court. Vista Jail was at least an hour or more away from the other jails so the problem was we needed to feed them their hot dinner up there before they were bussed home for the night.

My staff and I got together and came up with a solution. We would put the dinners into 3 compartment tinfoil trays, just like the meals I used to make for Meals on Wheels programs in hospitals. The tray contained the hot food and the cold items were put into small paper bags. We shipped them up to the jail and fed the inmates before sending them back to their home jails.

We immediately started getting *compliments* from the inmates. They liked the "cook" at the Vista Jail better than the one where they were housed. The ironic part was that most of them came from old Central Jail and it was the same food we served to them there. The difference was the fact that the hot food was really hot and the cold food was really cold. Thus was born the first pre-pack system in Corrections; it was the same system being used widely in many School and Health Care institutions. Eventually I put the pre-pack program into all of the jails and increased not only the cost control but also the acceptance level of the inmates.

I had another small problem; Vista's kitchen renovation was scheduled to be done all wrong. The design had the scullery and dish machine area not only put in backwards but right in the path of the only way in and out of the kitchen. Not being known for shyness, I told the Lieutenant in charge of the renovation that it was all wrong and needed to be changed. He became very upset and said that it was too late and would cost a lot of money to change it now. (At the time I was new and he didn't know my experience level.)

So I told him I would wait until it was finished; after the mistakes had been rectified, I would open the kitchen. (Not that I am stubborn or anything) That is exactly what I did; when they gave me the new kitchen I put all the inmates on meals sent from Central and made the kitchen workable and safe to use before it was opened for business.

Needless to say, I thought the Lieutenant would hate me forever. However, we went on from there and designed three more jails together and he forgave me. It was a good thing because he gradually rose in rank to two above me and high in the command. He did great things for the Sheriff's Department and wound up helping me in my job to keep everything going well in foodservices. You should always try not to tick anyone off if you can help it; you never know what is in the future.

They did not want me to become bored so a few months later my boss presented us with another challenge. Since our system was terribly over crowded, we were going to add a temporary 650 bed men's jail next to Las Colinas, our women's jail. We needed to find a way to feed them. The women's jail was old and originally designed as a 150 bed camp for girls. We had 850 women in the jail and we were finding it difficult enough to feed them; no way could we add 650 more mouths to feed out of that kitchen. It would be like if I gave you 50 people to feed out of your home kitchen.

We decided to go into Cook/Chill a little early. We put a Blast Chiller in Central Jail and we produced all the hot food for Central plus the 2 jails at Las Colinas. We chilled the food and then pre-packed the meals into tinfoil trays. Since making sure the inmates all get the same amount of each item is extremely important, pre-packing their meals came in handy. The inmates were a lot about *size*; the one who gets the biggest piece of cake or the biggest banana will wind up in a fight to keep it.

I took care of the bananas by ordering green tip bananas which had a certain amount to a stem and were all the same size. All the cakes, pies and sweetbreads were cut so each piece was the same size as well. Of course we supervised the tray line to assure accuracy.

I bought my first 24 foot refrigerated truck and we shipped the meals to Las Colinas 5 days a week. They rethermed the meals (brought the food up to temperature) at the jail. In the meantime, I wanted to give the female inmate workers something to do so I put a small bakery operation in their kitchen. They made all the desserts, rolls and sweet breads for both jails. When our driver dropped off the meals, he picked up the bakery goods for Central.

We learned to watch for notes the female inmates put in the pans or shipping racks to the male inmates in the other jail. After all, the large pool of males who probably moved in their same social circles was irresistible to them.

When I explained what we were going to do to my staff I could see that they thought I was crazy. I had two great Assistant Chiefs, Mr. Paul Benitez and Mr. Hans Ludwig, both retired Navy Chiefs, as well as some outstanding Food Service Supervisors. I was blessed that they all helped me develop this system, by much trial and error, and thank God it worked. It really got us ready for the Production Center that I was busy designing during this time.

We made every mistake in the book but quickly learned from them and moved on. Two things resulted from doing this system; the cost of the inmate meals went down <u>20 percent</u> for these three jails and the inmates stopped complaining about the food. This told us we were on the right track!

One of my favorite jails was a medium security facility out in the mountains. It was an old Japanese war camp and had been converted to a jail for about 500 inmates. It was absolutely beautiful out there and even got snow in the winter which seemed weird as it was less than an hour from the beach. In the winter, in Southern California, I had jails that were actually snowed in for a while but we handled it and no one ever missed a meal.

The inmates were housed in dorms with more freedom to move around. On a typical day, you would see them playing baseball surrounded by large pine trees under a perfect blue sky. They had a gardening group who grew beautiful roses and a cactus garden. It was a privilege to be there for inmates and staff alike. They all had to be on their best behavior or they were sent down to a high security facility where you didn't see the light of day very much.

The kitchen was in terrible shape with equipment older than me so I made it a top priority to do something about it. What I did was tear it apart inside. We put in new equipment and painted and cleaned it for two months. In the meantime, we operated off the back covered porch area and mainly barbequed everything. The guys *loved* it; they said it was a lot like camping. You know how guys like to grill and camp so I did not receive any complaints.

A few incidents stick out in my memory about this jail. We sometimes housed illegal aliens for the Feds. On one occasion, they were all Chinese and they were going to Medical in droves, complaining about pain in their stomachs. It seems the food did not agree with them as they had just got here from China. I told the cooks to give them 2 cups of steamed rice with every meal. We didn't hear a word out of them after that. I told the Sergeant in charge to tell them that the next time they break into a country to commit crimes, break into one where they like the food; it would be a lot easier on everyone.

Remember the cactus garden I told you about? Well, we had one problem with it. For a while, the inmates were into using the cactus needles to tattoo themselves. Many of them had infections and needed medical care. It wasn't too bad until they decided to tattoo their private parts. Talk about idiots! Some of them had to be in the hospital for a long while and some came out with less than what they went in with, if you get my drift. Word got around and it wasn't as popular any more. Do you know anywhere else, besides jail, where cactus needles are contraband?

MAPLE NUT SWEET BUNS

These buns came to be called "Miss Louise's Sweet Buns". There was an incident in one of our jails shortly after we started making these sweet buns for breakfast. The inmates were playing cards in the day room and using the sweet buns in place of money. Some of them had quite a pile of them.

In another part of the day room, about 10 inmates got into a fight so the deputies sounded the alarm to lock down and ordered all the inmates back into their cells. The inmates with the most sweet buns couldn't carry them all and wouldn't go to their cells. They actually had to break out the riot gear and weapons to get them to comply. When the inmates were finally let out of their cells, a few at a time, there was almost *another* riot because the first ones to be let out took the sweet buns and ate them.

I was teased without mercy for a long time that the inmates would not leave my "sweet buns" behind for anything. You have to find humor where you can when working behind bars and when you are the "butt" of it, take it graciously.

*Note: In the jail we made sweet yeast dough and used it instead of the packaged rolls in this recipe. You can make sweet dough as well if you have the time and patience but this is an easy and quick way to make this recipe. You can also make it with pecans instead of peanuts or no nuts at all. Anyway you do it; your family will love them just as well. I like to do things quick and easy if possible, especially in the morning when I am making these for breakfast. I defy you to eat only one!

Preheat oven to 350 degrees

- I stick, (4 ounces) butter
- I cup brown sugar
- ¼ cup maple syrup
- I cup roasted peanuts, chopped
- 2 packages crescent rolls

1. Whip the butter, brown sugar and maple syrup together until light and fluffy. Spread evenly on a cookie sheet.
2. Sprinkle peanuts on top of the mixture.
3. Remove the crescent rolls from the package, roll each one up into a crescent and lay them on top of the mixture.
4. Bake at 350 degrees for 20-30 minutes or until golden brown.
5. Cool for about 5 minutes and then remove them from the pan and place sticky side up on a serving platter. These are great warm or cold but I like them warm.

To give you an example, the Original Recipe was for 2500 sweet buns. It called for 15 pounds of butter, 45 pounds of brown sugar and 45 pounds of peanuts. We repeated this recipe 3 times for one serving day.

CHICKEN ADOBO (Serves 6-8)

This Filipino dish was very popular with the inmates/wards and staff even though there was less than 2% of Filipinos in jail. It appealed to all nationalities and age groups. It is very simple to make with just a few ingredients. You can use different flavors of vinegar such as red wine vinegar which will provide a subtle change to the taste. Since all we have is white vinegar in jail, we left it traditional which I prefer anyway. We also used boneless chicken thighs but you can use boneless chicken breasts or pieces of chicken as well. This dish does very well for potlucks as it holds up under heat and is very popular. Serve it with steamed rice, crusty bread and fruit to make a very satisfying "jail house" dinner.

- 3-4 pounds skinless, boneless chicken thighs
- 1 tablespoon vegetable oil
- 1 cup white vinegar
- ¾ cup soy sauce
- ½ teaspoon ground ginger
- 1 teaspoon sugar
- 4 cloves garlic, crushed
- 1 teaspoon black pepper
- 3 bay leaves

1. Heat the oil in a large skillet.
2. Lightly sauté the chicken for 2 minutes; remove and set aside.
3. Remove the oil and put the chicken back in the skillet.
4. Add the rest of the ingredients and bring to a boil.
5. Cover and let simmer for 20 minutes, stirring occasionally.

6. Uncover and simmer until the sauce is reduced and the chicken is tender, about 20 minutes.

7. Remove the bay leaves and serve with steamed rice.

UGLY DUCKING CAKE (Serves 8)

This cake was originally one of my family recipes and I brought it with me when I was the Food Service Director for schools. I also used it a lot when I did Hawaiian Luaus for catering events. We added a little green food coloring into the topping in Step 4 and decorated the cake with pineapple tops and cherries. In the jails, we served this cake about four times a year and always on Easter but we did not tint it green. (Inmates and children do not like eating *anything* green.) As we have to watch the nutrition levels for the inmates and this cake is basically a nightmare when it comes to sugar, fat and cholesterol, we didn't serve it more often. However, we did serve Pineapple Upside Down Cake about once a month in its place. You guessed it, everyone loved both cakes. I hope you enjoy it as well.

Preheat oven to 325 degrees

- 1 package yellow cake mix
- 3 large eggs
- ½ cup vegetable oil
- 1 can, (14.5 ounces) fruit cocktail, not drained
- 1 cup shredded coconut
- ½ cup brown sugar

Topping:
- ½ cup granulated sugar
- ½ cup (4 ounces) margarine or butter

- ½ cup evaporated milk
- I cup shredded coconut

1. In a mixer on medium speed combine the cake mix, eggs, oil, fruit cocktail and coconut; mix for 2 minutes until smooth.
2. Pour into a greased 9x12x2 inch pan. Top with brown sugar.
3. Bake at 325 degrees for about 45 minutes or until the top springs back when touched.
4. While the cake is baking, in a small pot bring the sugar, margarine and milk to a boil; boil 2 minutes.
5. Remove from the heat and add the coconut. Spoon over the hot cake.
6. The cake can be served warm or cold.

San Diego Jail Sample Menu:

Breakfast: Sliced melon, oatmeal, French toast, sausage, margarine, syrup and milk

Lunch: Minestrone soup and crackers, ham and cheese sandwich, shredded lettuce, pasta salad, peanut butter cookie, fruit and punch.

Dinner: Chicken Adobo, rice, mixed vegetables, dinner roll and margarine, garden salad with dressing, Ugly Duckling Cake and punch.

PRUNO

Pruno is a form of liquor that the inmates make in their cells or in the kitchen; they do this all over the world in jails with minor variations. Basically, they put together bread, sugar and fruit. They really prefer straight yeast instead of bread but we lock that up in "hot storage" just for this reason.

They usually put everything in a plastic bag and tie it up. The bag is put away to ferment, usually in their toilets. (Yes, this is not a misprint) Some people will do anything for booze! The deputies usually find it as (DUH) they know where to look.

They also find other warm places to hide it. One time they took the large cover off the ice machine motor, stuffed in the bag and replaced the cover. That would have worked if the motor didn't shut down due to a lack of air circulation. The inmates were not happy when we gave it to the deputy and he took it away, smacking his lips, in jest, as he went.

We had an incident where the kitchen inmates made Pruno in the old Central Jail kitchen when the cook wasn't looking and hid it in the air vent in the storeroom. We had a week of 100 degree weather and by the time they drank some, it was really spoiled but they were too lit to care. Because it is nice to share, they also put some on the food carts to go down to the floors for the inmate workers to drink. All in all, there were 30 really sick inmates!

I was at home fixing dinner and I had the news on TV. I looked up and saw one of my cooks holding a food tray that had a sign on it that said, "Dead Man's Tray". I almost had a heart attack. Let me explain. We have a sample tray from every meal that is saved in the refrigerator for three days in case of any problems. They label it "Dead Man's Tray". From that day on, they were told to use "Sample Tray" for obvious reasons. You can go to almost any jail in the world and you will see their "Dead Man's Tray".

The reporter was saying that 30 inmates had become deathly ill from food poisoning and that the incident was being investigated. I was lead story for three days; it must have been a slow news week. All the meal components were sent to the Health Department to be analyzed. Of course it had to be a hamburger, macaroni and cheese and vegetable meal; meat and cheese spoil or become contaminated very easily. All the items came out OK in the end. In fact, the Health

Department Director called me directly and she asked me what I had done to the macaroni and cheese.

I had my heart in my throat until she explained. It seems that it didn't even have bacteria that *should have* been in it. It was like I had washed it with soap or something. I explained to her that we used cook/chill technology to prepare the macaroni and cheese and the process kills or retards bacteria making the food safe to keep and eat.

We all knew that it was the Pruno the inmates had made and drank that made them ill. The first inmates to get sick were the ones in the kitchen who drank the most and they were so sick they thought they were going to *die* so they confessed what had happened immediately. However, we still had to be sure and go through all the procedures we have in place to insure the inmates safety as much as possible. I was teased forever about what happened but alls' well that ends well.

Inmates, no matter how old they are, have a lot of ingenuity, especially when it comes to getting high. For example, the male wards at one of our Juvenile camps in the mountains were repeatedly caught smoking so the officers went looking for the source since it wasn't tobacco. It seems that they were pulling weeds from behind their dormitory and smoking them. The wards were made to completely clean the fields of weeds and keep them clean and that solved the problem. The things you learn in jail!

*Note: Hot storage is a locked, caged area where we put the yeast and all the spices. Believe it or not, if you sniff nutmeg you can get quite high; so who knew? You can also smoke anything green. In a jail in Tennessee, the Sheriff ordered that spinach be taken off the menu as the inmates were drying it and then smoking it. I can honestly say that I never removed a food from a menu if the inmates were abusing it. We just increased our security.

Chapter 6

San Diego Goes Modern; A Dream Come True

"Watch yourself about complaining.
If you don't like a thing, change it;
if you can't change it, change the way you feel about it.
Don't complain."
—*Maya Angelou*

I want you to picture this scenario. Every day, at 2:00 am, we dragged a bunch of inmates, mainly unsentenced felons, out of bed in each jail and directed them in preparing meals for thousands of other inmates. The ratio of Sheriff's cooks to inmates was one to fifteen. The inmates were mostly inexperienced, didn't want to be there and some were downright mean.

Even though this is par for the course in jails, I hated it; this was a recipe for disaster! I wanted to provide good quality, cost effective meals for the inmates which was an entirely new idea. There was no use complaining so I decided to change it. It was impossible to guarantee the quality, safety and consistency of the meals if we still did status quo. This explained why there were so many inmate complaints, disturbances and law suits due to the food before I got there; because of this they agreed to consider my recommendation to consolidate the foodservices.

My plan was to build a facility which utilized inmate labor in supporting tasks, not cooking or baking the food. This would assure not only the quality and safety of the food but also preserve the integrity of the equipment while still utilizing inmate labor.

In 1989, we were getting ready to build two jails out in the boondocks in Otay Mesa next to the Mexican border. I really didn't want to build my big kitchen all the way out there but at least I had land and an existing budget already in place which is half the battle.

They had to cut the top off a small mountain in order to build on that site. I literally pictured the big warehouse type buildings sitting on top of the cleared space, shining in the sun. So I requested a "few million" more to build a centralized production center.

I had no idea that it was usually next to impossible to get the Sheriff, the CEO of the County *and* the Board of Supervisors to agree on anything, never mind something that was not ever done before in Corrections; somehow I succeeded. It made so much sense that I never envisioned *not doing it.*

Before they knew it, we had added a Central Laundry and Warehouse to the complex as well as maintenance services, a boiler plant and a gas station. The laugh was on me since I had to help design the warehouse and laundry. This was new to me but I had fun doing it. It certainly was easier than designing kitchens.

I had a real blast designing the Central Production Center. I visited all kinds of other food industry production plants and researched the newest and best equipment available at the time. I took ideas from this one and that one and added some of my own. I looked for ways to cut costs while designing a state of the art facility that was geared to make the employees work smart and happy as well.

I bugged manufacturers of high tech equipment to redesign their equipment to fit the needs of the production center and the receiving sites as well. For example, Bud Chambers with Cambro designed a cart for our jails to bring the pre-packed meals to the inmates. The team at Design Specialties, Jack, Pat, Pattie and Michael, designed, produced and supplied us with a special, reusable meal tray. John Mikulka, with Allan Packaging, facilitated the design of a bio-degradable paper meal tray for our diets. Roland and Susan with Cleveland provided equipment and expertise for the cook/chill system. These companies were wonderful to us and because of them we really succeeded beyond my expectations.

Since I had started using a new technology when I worked in school foodservice called "Cook /Chill", I proposed that we also use this method to safely manufacture the cooked food for all the jails. I went even further in proposing we serve the Juvenile Facilities as well as Children's Centers and Meals on Wheels Programs and any other County departments as well as catered events. I estimated that we would save over a million dollars a year for the Sheriff's Department alone which thank goodness turned out to be true.

In 1991, we opened the 38,000 square foot Sheriff's Central Production Center (CPC), manufacturing 33,000 meals a day; a one of a kind operation in Corrections. By 1996 we started to provide food and services to the Probation facilities and the Children's Center, saving these departments in excess of $700,000 a year. Ten years later, I added another 4,000 square feet in refrigerated/freezer space to support the now *43,000 meals* per day production schedule.

In 2003, a large Meals on Wheels Program lost their vendor. They were desperate to find someone to prepare meals for their 1400 senior citizens. Our wonderful Sheriff Bill Kolender, being very civic minded said, "Louise will take care of you." And so we did for the next two years.

We were already providing holiday meals for the County's Meals on Wheels program but this was an entirely new program that added 2,400 meals more a day, 7 days a week. My great staff rose to the occasion. We gave the seniors many of the meals that we gave the inmates, with a few variations such as stuffed cabbage which the inmates would hate but *they* liked; the seniors loved all the food!

We provided all the special medical diets as well since we already had a program in place for the inmates. I worked with the Meals on Wheels staff in developing their own program and in two years they went out on their own. They lost many of their clients because they missed their jail food which was a compliment to us but a problem for them. Their meals were not bad just different and as you know, no one likes change.

After a few years, everything worked out in the end for them. As they lost clients, they obtained new ones who did not have the jail food before and therefore did not miss it. It is so nice to be appreciated.

The CPC included the newest in technology, the Cook/Chill production method of preparing food. Food, such as stews, sauces, soups, gravy, hot cereal and chili is cooked to at least 180 degrees in large, 200 gallon mixer kettles and then pumped into special plastic barrier bags and sealed. The bags are dropped automatically into tumble chillers where they tumble around in cold water for about an hour until the temperature of the food drops to less than 40 degrees. This puts a shelf life of 4-6 weeks on the product.

The bags are placed in really cold refrigerators (33 degrees) until they are needed for the meals. You take out just what you need and the rest stays safely in the refrigerator until the next time. This cuts down on the food waste considerably.

If you were to go into the kitchens of some of the big chain restaurants, you would see the bags of food sitting in their refrigerators. They have central plants where the food is made for all their restaurants. This way your favorite chowder will be at all of their restaurants around the country. This saves them money and generates repeat customers; a win-win situation.

I added a large salad and vegetable production component that employed enormous cutting and dicing equipment and vegetable washers and dryers. All the tossed salads were made in this area; we bagged the salad in 5 or 10 pound bags and vacuum packed it. We processed approximately **670,000** pounds of lettuce annually. It now had a 1-2 week shelf life on it and the inmates and staff never had to eat brown or wilted salad.

We made thousands of pounds of potato salad, tuna salad, cole slaw and macaroni salad as well. In addition, this area prepared all the vegetables for the cooking areas such as potatoes, onions, carrots and celery, literally by the tons each week.

I put in a large, commercial bakery to produce the thousands of cookies, cakes, rolls, buns and French bread needed to feed our population. For instance, we made *2 million* cookies a year. It has huge mixers from Germany which you and I could fit in together, large double rack baking ovens, a cookie machine, a cake depositor and a roll and bread making system.

Everything was made from scratch with no preservatives using vegetable shortening and very little sodium. It not only made the meals more palatable but it was inexpensive to do. For instance, the cookies cost about $.03 each, the cake was $.05 per slice and the hamburger buns were $.80 a dozen. On *one* given day, we popped out **9,000** hamburger buns, **700** French bread, **8,500** pieces of cake and **10,000** cookies. Our rolls and bread were nothing short of heavenly; I really miss them.

San Diego was the first in the nation to incorporate all these activities under one roof for Correctional feeding. We also introduced the first pre-pack system of preparing and serving meals for jails. The entrée part of the meal is trayed and sealed at the CPC and then shipped to the 11 receiving sites; we packed 23,000 meals per day using inmate labor.

To quote from the article by Tom Dougherty, *Cook's Food Makes Peace in Prison*: 'The menu is low in fat and sodium and high in fresh fruits and vegetables. They eat better than they do at home; our goal is to get them healthy and keep them healthy. (Since we provide their medical care, it behooves us to do so). Mathews said that she works just as hard at making the food look good as she does making it nutritious. Everything is color and texture coordinated, she said. She says she loves cooking and advises people who do it only from a sense of duty to give it up.'

I do not remember saying the last statement but it sounds like me. I believe that you should do what you truly love to do if at all possible and to do it to the best of your ability. I value passion in all work, even above expertise! I can honestly say that I was always passionate about whatever I did.

I did not do all this for fame and glory but it happened anyway. I had such a supportive Sheriff Command staff that believed in us as well as the greatest, most devoted foodservice professionals anywhere making it all happen every day. We received great publicity and many awards; I personally received recognition beyond anything I ever envisioned.

In 1994 I received the Food Service Industry's highest honor; the IFMA Silver Plate Award. I was only the second person, as well as the first woman, in Corrections to get this award. In 1995, I was awarded an Honorary Doctorate of Foodservice by NAFM. Being presented with these two honors was the high light of my career!

The Central Production Center still sits today on the top of the hill, shining in the sun; it makes it all worthwhile.

THAI CHICKEN CURRY (Serves 6)

When we first started up our Production Center, we were blessed to have three fine, dedicated Food Service Supervisors; Ms Neila Afan-Cook, Mr. Mel Valenzuela and Mr. Joe Castro. They helped my Assistant Chiefs, Paul Benitez and Hans Ludwig and me develop and refine our recipes.

When we first tried to adapt this recipe for Cook/Chill to cook in our 200 gallon steam kettles and then chill it in bags to be served a week or two later, we ran into problems. It turned a hideous yellow and burned the skin off your lips. It seems that when you let spices sit for a while, they multiply. We already knew to reduce the spices but with this dish, the curry seemed to have a mind of its' own.

We finally got it where it would be acceptable to the majority of the 7000 people who ate it. Of course, some of our recipe testers liked the original recipe just fine but you have to please the majority, even, or especially, in jail.

We used skinless, boneless chicken thighs in our recipes as it held up well under the steam and stayed moist. Most of the juveniles would not like it no matter *how* we cooked it so they received something else that day, like maybe liver. (I am only kidding about the liver. No one likes liver; they used to serve it in jail before I got there and almost no one EVER ate it.)

*Note: We could not afford to do this in jail but you can add ½ cup golden raisins and/or chopped dried apricots. You also can substitute ¾ cup of coconut milk and 1 cup of plain yogurt for the chicken broth, for a really traditional dish. If you do not like a lot of "heat", use only 2 tablespoons of curry powder.

- 3 tablespoons olive or vegetable oil
- 2 raw chicken breasts cut in pieces
- I onion, chopped
- I green or red pepper cut in strips
- 3 garlic cloves, minced
- 3 tablespoons curry powder
- I teaspoon paprika
- I teaspoon salt
- I teaspoon black pepper
- I teaspoon cinnamon
- ½ teaspoon ground ginger
- I teaspoon sugar

- 1 can, (14 ounces) chicken broth
- Cooked rice, white or brown

1. Heat the oil in a large pan. Sauté the chicken until light brown. Remove the chicken.
2. Add the onion, peppers and garlic to the pan and cook until lightly browned.
3. Add the curry powder, mix well. Add the other spices and sugar, cook one minute; stir well.
4. Place the chicken on top of the mixture. Add the broth.
5. Partially cover the pot and simmer for about 10-15 minutes until the chicken is cooked through. Serve over rice.

SPANISH RICE (Yields 8 cups)

This is a very popular side dish that is easy to make and goes with just about anything such as burritos and enchiladas. We also served this rice with scrambled eggs, refried beans and tortillas for breakfast. What I like about it is that it is the moist kind of Spanish rice, not the dry kind. We made it this way at the jail because we were using cook/chill where you heat the rice up again at a later date. The dry version of this dish did not take well to reheating. We tried to serve our food at the optimum taste as well as texture. I used to get teased that this is why some of our "customers" were repeat visitors.

- 3 tablespoons vegetable oil
- ¼ medium onion, chopped
- 1 tablespoon minced garlic
- 4 cups white rice
- 6 cups chicken broth

- 2 cups crushed tomatoes
- I tablespoon salt
- I tablespoon pepper

1. Heat oil in a large pot.
2. Sauté the onion and garlic until translucent.
3. Add the rice and allow it to get light brown, stirring constantly.
4. Add the chicken broth and bring to a boil.
5. Add all other ingredients and bring back to a boil.
6. Reduce the heat, partially cover and simmer for about 20 minutes, stirring occasionally.
7. You can add 1 cup of frozen mixed vegetables in step 5 to make a complete vegetable dish. You also can add a little red pepper or Tabasco sauce to make it spicier.

A WORD ABOUT TOMATO SAUCE

All jails have tomato sauce in some form and they serve it with various kinds of pasta. They all have some kind of tomatoes in it and usually garlic and onions but that is where the similarity ends. You would think that this would be easy, right?

I saw one recipe where they used tomato paste, water, green peppers and some catsup for flavoring. You can imagine how gross it tasted and looked. There is simply no reason not to do it correctly. It takes almost as much effort to do it wrong as it takes to do it right.

Tomato sauce is used on top of almost everything in jails and they then think that it makes it "I—talian". They serve it on all kinds of stuff like soy patties, vegetables, and chicken, pork, beef and fish patties. They even mix it with canned beef and serve it for breakfast. This is called Minced Beef. It is an old military recipe and we served it for years during the winter in San Diego; the male inmates liked it, "the women not so much".

In Corrections, most menu items are governed by budget and time constraints. Everything is run on a tight schedule, assuring that the inmates are fed before the courts start; the judges tend to get cranky when they are late.

In addition, regulations dictate how much time is allowed between meals in California. Not more than 14 hours shall pass between meals without supplemental food being offered to the inmates. They must have three meals per day, at least one of them being hot. You can see that a lot of things come in play when working out the menus and when they will be cooked and served.

Therefore, using easy, universally accepted foods like tomato sauce, goes a long way in helping us achieve all of our goals.

An absolute favorite of the inmates was pizza of any kind. We made our pizza for years using our tomato sauce, pizza dough placed on 18x26 sheet pans and shredded cheese. During my last few years at work we could actually get frozen pre-portioned square pan style pizza that was quite good and inexpensive. Most of our customers didn't know the difference. Believe me, if they did, I would hear about it. They have nothing else to do but pick their food apart and write to us.

Pizza can be very nutritious, depending on what you put on it and is popular with everyone so don't be afraid to make it and serve it to your family, even for breakfast. I love pineapple, cheese and turkey ham which is perfect for breakfast or any time.

I suggest that you make extra tomato sauce and freeze it; always have on hand canned or frozen dough and grated mozzarella cheese. With the addition of veggies or leftover meats, it won't take long to put together a meal that pleases everyone.*Note: In San Diego, we used DAD'S TOMATO GRAVY recipe, in Chapter 1, as our base for our tomato sauce.

Chapter 7

This and That

When I works, I work hard.
When I sits, I sit loose.
When I thinks, I fall asleep.
—*Anon*

As we go through life we encounter many challenges and unusual situations which shape and enrich our lives. The trick is to learn from them and flavor everything with humor. Here are some of the things that happened to me; they helped me when I finally wound up working in jail.

The Floating Pig: In 1980, I was running the Food Service for an Elks Lodge in Virginia. A *thousand* men and me; what a chore! It was a *no women allowed* club except on certain days. Every time I came into the bar or the dining room, these Southern gentlemen would all stand up; it took me months to break them of it.

I never went into the card room, I just used the intercom system to talk to them; it was *sacred* in there. Some of the wives would call for them and of course the guys would say that they weren't there. The wives would give me a message for when they would decide to show up; for instance, "take your medicine" or "get home to supper by 6:00pm or else".

Some of my customers were quite elderly but still spry; my best boyfriend was 98 years old! Little did I know that in my future lay the jails with even more thousands of men to feed but they were not my type.

Since I was the first female to be a manager of their Elks Lodge as well as the *only* female manager on that coast, it was rough in the beginning to prove myself. Some of them would say, "You are a pretty little thing but don't you think you should be at home with your husband and your children?"

The first day I worked there, my cooking and wait staff, who were all African American, gave me two weeks' notice. I asked them to give me a chance to prove myself and if they still wanted to leave in a month, I would understand. They never left and we had a good time providing food services to the lodge brothers. I found out later that they said they were leaving just in case I was going to fire them.

My main cook, Miss Annie, was a treasure. She never looked like she was moving very much but got everything done. I learned to stay out of her way and let her ask me for help in her off-handed way. She also taught me a few things about Southern cooking.

One day I put Yankee Pot Roast on the menu and the brother Elks caused such a fuss, I had to take it off the menu board and rename it Southern Pot Roast; I was informed by Miss Annie that is what it *really* was *anyway*. She would instruct me and then walk away muttering her favorite expression, "Lord, take me closer to the Cross".

On another occasion, I put Chicken and Dumplings on the menu for the Kiwanis's Club, for about 100 people. When I peeked into the kitchen about a half hour before they were due to arrive, I saw Miss Annie and two of the waiters hurrying about and not nearly done yet. When I asked what the problem was Miss Annie mumbled to the air that "some Northerners don't know much about cooking. Mmm, mmm, mmm!" (Another of her favorite expressions)

You see, I thought she dropped the dumpling batter into the pan of boiling chicken and gravy like I did but I learned that any self respecting Southern cook would roll her dumplings like *she* was having to do and for a 100 men to boot! She was a lot "closer to the cross" that day and I learned to put the menu by her first for her approval.

I did manage to teach Miss Annie a few things I knew about

cooking that impressed her. For a French Buffet, I taught her how to make Coquille St. Jacques. She thought it was really something. I also taught her how to cook real Mexican food which was kind of a novelty at that time in Virginia.

I talked my way into that job by promising them that I would put in a catering program which would pay off their mortgage and I did that very thing. However, I almost lost my credibility one night during a violent, unexpected rain storm.

We were doing a "Pig Picken" the next day and in Virginia you bury the pig in a pit and roast it the *right* way. I left a worker there to watch the pig which they thought was a funny thing to do until the rains came. I got a frantic call in the middle of the night that the pit was flooded and the pig was floating and threatening to wash away. So I went down there and we hauled it out, took it apart so it would fit in the ovens and roasted it.

There were many "Oh, Lordy me and please save us" that night. They all thought I was nuts. We put the pig back together, decorating it carefully to hide the places where we cut it and the "Pig Picken" was a big success. They said it was the best one ever. Everyone was sworn to secrecy and thank God they never told on me. I have done many whole pigs since then in other places and I made sure I had big enough ovens so they would fit, just in case.

I had to leave that job after two years due to my Navy husband being transferred to California. The men collected $650 for a divorce so I could stay with them. They also bought me a set of luggage in case I still wanted to leave. I really did not want to leave that job.

They were the sweetest bunch of men I ever had an occasion to meet. We had a group of musicians with an average age of 65 years old (I thought that was *old* in those days) that played for many of our functions. They always played, *Don't You Make my Brown Eyes Blue*, just for me and when I heard it, I had to come and sit with the piano player so he could sing it to me. Every time I hear the song, I think of them. (Many inmates sang for us in jail but with no piano and I didn't sit with them. It just wasn't the same.)

Jailbirds Order up Hot Wings; taken from the Wall Street Journal, April 27, 2010.

In some jails, extra food is offered at a price for those who can afford it. ARAMARK, a large food service contractor, supplies food services to the Indiana State Prisons. They also sell the inmates different food for $7-$12 for a hot meal to $100 for a junk food box filled with beef jerky, iced cookies, vanilla cappuccino or other goodies not available in the commissary.

The Correctional facility gets a percentage of the profits. Pizza and hot wings, jumbo cheeseburger and fries, cheese and beef nachos and jalapeno poppers are just a few of the meals offered to the inmates. One inmate said that in four months, his sister has spent close to $1,000 ordering him junk food. "Sometimes it feels like it's not even jail. Jail's supposed to be bread and water", he said.

All I can say is thank God he was over 18 or the School Lunch Program would kick in and he would never see *any* of that food; I don't care how much money his sister had!

THINGS YOU LEARN THE HARD WAY

We all have a list of things we have learned the hard way and my list is long. For instance, when cooking, do not reach into a deep oven without protection on your arms or you get *cook's hash marks*. When trying to light a burner which has gone out, do not put your hair close to the burner; ditto for your sleeves or dish towels. I know for a *fact* they all catch fire. Mama didn't raise no fool.

Listen to the inmates. We all learned to listen to the inmates and filter out the garbage to get to what we should know. I received a complaint from a Hispanic inmate which said he hated to complain but the chili was "too damn hot". This interested me so I went to see him. I asked him if he had trouble with his stomach or did he normally eat spicy food. He told me he loved spice but my chili was *really* hot. I told him I would check on it and I did.

He was right; my cooks had tested the chili when they cooked it but then it was chilled and it sat in the refrigerator for a few days before heating and serving it. We had just started doing Cook/Chill and we were still learning how much the spices multiply. We corrected the recipe and I sent a response to the inmate, thanking him for telling me.

In another instance, we heard through the inmate hot line, from the female kitchen workers, one of the inmates was taking worms out of the garden and putting them in her food. She would do this when she was almost finished eating, make a big fuss and would then be given another tray. She was moved to a unit where she did not have access to worms anymore and that solved the problem.

Susan Madden Lankford, who is a photographer, was shooting pictures for her book about female inmates. This inmate told her about finding a maggot in her sweet potatoes. (As everyone knows, sweet potatoes do not normally form maggots) However, Susan liked it so much she made it the title of her book: Maggots *in My Sweet Potatoes: Women Doing Time.*

Of course, I made sure we toured Susan through our kitchen at the jail as well as our Production Center and she could see the cleanliness and the care we took with the food. She acknowledged as much when she was interviewed in the newspaper but still liked and kept the title. The book is very well done but I would have preferred a different title.

Do not go into an unlit jewelry store. I was on my way home from work and I needed to pick something up. I walked into the jewelry store and didn't realize the lights were off until I was half way inside. I noticed one guy behind the counter on the left with a white tee shirt and ball cap. Two others were in front of the counter dressed the same way but the man standing behind the right hand counter really got my attention. He was holding a large gun that was pointed straight at me.

I slowly turned around and started back out. He yelled at me; "Hey, Lady! Get back here or I'll blow your f… head off". Since he put it that way, I had no choice. I had a big problem; as I had just come from work, I still had my badge on. I was afraid if he saw it, he *would* shoot me.

I asked him what he wanted. He said he wanted me to come closer to him so I did, looking him in the face the entire time for two reasons. The first reason was to keep him from noticing my badge; the second reason was I was memorizing his face so I could ID him in case I got out of this alive.

He had three people on the floor behind the counter; a man and two women, one of which was losing it big time. He kept yelling at her to stop crying. I was talking to him, asking him what he wanted. He said he wanted me on the other side of the counter and to jump over it. Up to this point, I was ready to cooperate.

I explained to him I had a dress on and I would have to go all the way over to the other side of the room, where the other guys were stuffing jewelry into pillow cases, to get a running start. I asked him to open the door on the counter. He couldn't figure out the latch; he started to get so nervous his hands started to shake. I was afraid he would shoot me accidentally so I offered to crawl under the counter.

I had forgotten about my ample derriere; it was a tight squeeze but I made it. He had me lie down on my face and jabbed me in the back of the head with the gun, screaming that if I moved he would f…shoot me. No problem; I couldn't even breathe, never mind move.

I tried to calm down the girl beside me. The male employee whispered that he didn't think it was a real gun. Since I had been staring down the barrel for awhile, I said I knew it was real and not to move. We felt the floor shaking as they started to run out of the store. Then the gun went off; I thought that if it happened again I would crawl towards the back door. But he was only firing it to keep us from chasing him, thank God. I waited a few minutes and then called Mall security, told them what happened and we immediately had a dozen security and law enforcement people respond.

The men got into a car and went to downtown San Diego, where they crashed into several cars. While they were trying to run away, the jewelry was spread all over the streets. It turned out they were all under 18 except the guy with the gun who turned 18 that day. Of course, it was drug related; they were stealing the jewelry to give to the gang leader in Los Angeles.

I did go to a lineup and identified the gunman. I was the only one who clearly saw his face. We also had some great fingerprints where he tried to open the door. Don't these guys ever watch TV? When they learned that a Sheriff was one of the victims, they all plead guilty and were sentenced to prison. What a waste of young lives. I was calm during the event but later that night, I could not stop shaking. It took a few years before I would go into a jewelry store again and I have never been able to go back to that particular store.

Never go out of a hotel room unless fully dressed. I was up in Northern California doing a consulting job for a Sheriff's Department and staying in the only hotel in town. I had dinner when I got in and three hours later it all wanted to come out. Since I had to stay up anyway to wait to feel better, I figured I would do my ironing for the 5 days I would be there. I called for an iron and the clerk reminded me that there was an one hour limit on the iron as they only had three irons; it was midnight so who else would want an iron?

I got the ironing done on time anyway and put the iron and board outside the door as requested. I noticed that the cord was too far out in the hallway so I used my foot to get it closer to me. You guessed it; as I was leaning out, the door closed behind me.

So, there I was, dressed only in a short nightgown, locked out of my room at 1:00 in the morning with a bad stomach ache. What would you have done? I knew I couldn't just stand there so I went to the nearest room to me and knocked on the door. No answer. I tried the other rooms around me and no luck. Then I saw a woman's arm come out of a room down the hall and hang a breakfast order on the door. I ran down there and knocked on the door; of course she didn't answer. I yelled through the door, "I know you are in there; I have locked myself out of my room; please call down stairs to have someone come and let me in my room". I ran quickly back and put my back against the door to wait.

It was only a minute when I heard the elevator; a security guard came out and walked down to me. He gave me a weird look and said, "We have had some complaints about a woman soliciting people and disturbing them." I asked him if he thought it was *me*? He said, "You *are* the one dressed in a short sexy nightgown". I explained I had got locked out of my room and to please let me in. He didn't seem to believe me so I told him I was with the San Diego Sheriff and was here doing a job for *their* Sheriff. He finally let me in the room.

My nightmare was not over. When I got into work the next morning, the sheriffs were all waiting for me and howling with laughter. It seems the security guard was a retired sheriff and had told everyone what happened; it was a long time before I lived it down.

Not Too Bright but All True

You can't make up some of the things that happen with criminals but you can learn from their mistakes.

A guy walks into a bank and demands to see the bank manager. He tells the manager that he has a bomb and that he wants $2,000 in unmarked bills. The manager tells him, "Certainly, Sir; that will not be a problem. Just fill out Form 282 and we will get it ready for you." While the bank robber is filling out the form, the cops are called. While he is being arrested, the manager calmly takes the form and puts "jail" in the address space. I like that guy!

Mr. X, a Florida resident, was the victim of a house burglary. The thieves ignored his wide screen TV, Rolex watch and other goodies. However, they did take a generic white box filled with a grayish-white powder. The police said it looked similar to high grade cocaine and the thieves had probably thought they had hit the big time.

Mr. X went on TV and pleaded with the burglars: 'Please return the cremated remains of my sister, Gertrude'. The next morning, the bullet ridden corpse of a local drug dealer was left on Mr. X's doorstep with the half empty box of ashes. A note said: "Hoochie sold us the bogus blow, so we wasted him. Sorry we snorted your sister. No hard feelings. Have a nice day."

In jail, we have a housing unit called the "snitch tank". This is the place where we house inmates who rat out other inmates or give evidence in court so we can keep them safe from retribution. In the kitchen, their meal cart is packed by a Sheriff's cook and padlocked. When the cart gets to the floor, the deputy unlocks the cart and puts it in their tank.

On this one particular day the cart wasn't in the tank 5 minutes when the inmates starting yelling and screaming that people were trying to kill them. When the deputy got there, a few inmates had their heads in the toilets and others were saying they were sick. It seems that the meals had been contaminated with *smelly stuff*. Some inmates were sent to Medical to be examined where they refused to have their stomachs pumped. They just wanted a lawyer so they could sue. That gave us our first clue.

When it came right down to it we found out that two of the inmates had taken "stuff" out of the toilet and smeared it on some of the food. No one actually ate the food; they just looked at it and threw up. An inmate in the tank snitched on them; what else would they expect since (Duh) they are in *snitch* tank. The two guilty inmates now had two years in *prison* tacked on to their sentence.

One sad commentary on the way our society works is people have been known to commit crimes just to *get into jail* so they can get free medical care, dental care, housing and food. For instance, we had one prostitute that had very bad teeth. Every time she was in jail they would treat her and eventually she had very few teeth left as she didn't take care of her teeth on the outside. The next time she was booked into jail, she went to see the dentist and demanded false teeth.

Since she was only in for a month this wasn't possible. She kicked such a fit saying we owed her false teeth; I have no idea where she gets this *owed* thing. So…she figured out a way to get into jail for a good amount of time; she threatened the arresting officers with a knife and accidentally cut one of them. The bad news was that she got prison time for this mess but the good news was she got her false teeth.

In another case there was a 62 year old man who had bad kidneys due to a life time of drinking and was on dialysis. He had been in and out of jail for several years and knew the ropes. The only problem was that this time he came in we were severely overcrowded; his crime was minor so he was booked and released. He was *not happy*; he needed to come back in for treatment.

He knew he needed to do a bigger crime so he tried to rob a liquor store but they threw him out and locked the door. So he got a fake gun, went up on the roof and tried to break in through the ventilation system. He fell through the ceiling, landing on the owner, breaking his leg and getting shot in the side by the other employee who had a real gun. So here he is back again into custody after a few days in the hospital. He was complaining bitterly on how much *trouble* he had to go through just to get back in for his treatment. This time he didn't have to worry about being released for a while since as he too went to prison.

As I am writing this book, there has been a series of bank robberies in San Diego by senior citizens. A 71 year old man who said he robbed a bank downtown because he wanted to be returned to prison for the medical care plead guilty to a robbery charge. He had two prior convictions for bank robberies in the late 1990s. One of these times, the cops didn't catch him fast enough so he called in and gave himself up so he could get back in jail for treatment.

This time around he used a wheelchair and a BB gun to rob the bank and left the bank with $2,000 in his lap. He was easy to catch; he was rolling down the street when 5 minutes later, the police arrested him about 4 blocks from the bank. He was happy to be back with us as his health problems—diabetes, gout, colon cancer, heart disease and glaucoma—were too much for him to handle on his own. It is amazing he could still pull off the robbery!

I received a call from the Sheriff's attorney one day. It seemed that an inmate that we had incarcerated for only four days was in the preliminary process of suing the county because his *foot fell off*. He was a diabetic and he contended that he wasn't served a diabetic diet while he was with us and this was why he lost his foot. Even though any *sane* person knows that 4 days without a diet isn't going to cause your foot to fall off, we had to answer up.

I presented documentation that he was indeed given the proper diet as soon as he was booked and that he also received his insulin shots. His lawyer withdrew the complaint. (Really?)

Even though only 10% of the inmates in jail are on diets, they cause most of the problems and extra work for food services. Along with medical diets, we provided genuine and verified religious diets. Religious diets cost a lot more than the regular meals with Kosher being the most expensive.

We had a system to identify those inmates who needed to be on a religious diet and provided these diets accordingly. Kosher diets seemed to be the most popular diet to request; no, we did not have that many actual Jewish inmates at any one given time. However, we did have some inmates that wanted the diet anyway; here are some of my favorites.

I was only working for the Sheriff for a few months when I got my first request for a Kosher diet. Up to this time, they did not provide religious diets unless it was "court ordered". I went to see the inmate; he turned out to be a 78 year old man who was in for attempted murder. He was a small man, stooped and gray and could hardly walk. He was handcuffed to the wall and kept trying to kiss my hand. Since he hadn't been able to eat for over a day, he was very happy to see me.

It seems that in his nursing home he had lit candles for his mother and father who were killed in the war camps. Two old ladies kept blowing out the candles so he attacked them with a large stainless steel can opener that he got from the kitchen. They were slightly hurt in the confrontation.

After talking to him, there was no doubt in my mind that the inmate was a Kosher Jew. Since my belief is that if an inmate has a genuine need for a religious diet we should provide one to the best of our ability, I went to see the Captain of the facility and convinced him I needed to do this diet. He kindly provided money out of petty cash so I could go and purchase some food. I quickly found a vender that could provide me frozen entrees that were Kosher.

A few weeks later, I received a call from a hospital where I had worked before going to jail. It seems that this inmate had been transferred there and would be with them for some time. He told them to call Mrs. Mathews in the jail and get his jail food as he wouldn't eat their food or take his medicine.

I told them, "I have such a deal for you!" I had all these frozen kosher meals just sitting in the freezer so I convinced my accounting people to make up an invoice, which was something new to them, and I sold the meals at cost to the hospital. The inmate now had his "jail food" and everyone was happy.

Some inmates who requested kosher meals did not get them and were not happy. One inmate said that his girlfriend was Jewish and she wanted him to eat Kosher. He was in jail for beating her senseless and she's worried about what he eats?

Another inmate said he wasn't really Jewish but he heard that Jews were smart and he needed all the help he could get when he went to court. I told him I agreed that he needed help but kosher food wasn't it. My favorite ones were the skin heads who *said* they were Kosher. They had all kinds of anti-Semitic tattoos all over their necks and bodies. The only synagogue they could name was the one they had burned down; you guessed it; not only no but *hell* no.

We had a serial killer from Chicago who was waiting for extradition back home who wanted a kosher diet. He was 400 pounds soaking wet and Italian. I went to see him; the deputies asked to leave him behind two sets of bars as he was a dangerous guy which was fine with me.

I had learned to talk to inmates just like I would talk to you and not think about why they were in jail. I introduced myself and said to him, "So, I hear you are from Chicago. I think they make the *best* pizza." He whole heartedly agreed with me. I asked him how he liked his pizza. He said, "I love lots of pepperoni and extra cheese." I said, "You are no more kosher than I am; you can't eat meat and dairy together. Why in the world do you want a kosher diet?"

With a sheepish grin he said that I was right, he wasn't Jewish but he was afraid that someone in the kitchen would try to kill him. (I can't understand why he would think that) I assured him that his food would be sent down in a special cart so no one could get at it. I included his tray on the snitch tank's cart and the deputies got it for him. I told him he didn't want to miss our great Italian food as kosher food is kind of bland.

He was happy with that and wanted to show me the rest of his tattoos that were in places I didn't want to think about but I declined. The deputies were happy too as he finally stopped bugging them.

My very favorite kosher inmate was a 350 pound chef who came in and out of our jail over a period of three years. He wrote me every week, requesting all sorts of reassurances that all the food he was receiving was kosher. We showed him the labels off the cans and boxes of food such as the crackers, Jello-o and canned fruits so he could see for himself.

He told me that his mother was disappointed in him. When I asked if it was because he was in jail, he said no. She was upset because he chose to be only a *chef.*

I had the orthodox Rabbi that visited Jewish inmates come in with me to talk to this guy. He told the inmate that he should be thankful that I was taking such pains to do what we could for him and the inmate said that he was very grateful. I loved that rabbi; he was really cool. It didn't stop the inmate from writing me every time he came into our jail. He had been sent to prison where they were not so accommodating but he kept coming back to us when he was a witness against other inmates in court. He loved his jail food.

I think the best diet ever requested while I was there was from two inmates that said that their religion (that didn't have a name) stated that the only food they could eat was steak and beer. I told them that I guess that they were going to starve then. I never got a reply back; what a surprise!

MR. Z'S FISH CHOWDER (8-10 servings)

We used to make this chowder to use up our extra fish for our staff at the Production Center. We named it for Mr. Z who started out as a Deputy, eventually went to Sheriff's Captain and then became a Commander and my boss. (It is a good thing he liked our food) He went up even higher before he retired and always supported us. He was a great guy who loved this great chowder so we named it after him.

Serve this hearty chowder with a simple salad and of course French or Italian bread for a great meal.

- ½ cup raw bacon, diced
- 1 medium onion, chopped
- 1 stalk celery, diced
- 1 bay leaf
- 6 small potatoes, diced
- 2 cups water
- 1 tablespoon clam base or salt
- 1 ½ pounds boneless, skinless white fish, cubed
- 1 ¼ quarts milk, regular or low fat
- 1 teaspoon white pepper
- 1 teaspoon Tabasco sauce

1. Cook the bacon until brown in a large pot.
2. Add the onion, celery and bay leaf; sauté for 5 minutes.
3. Add the potatoes, water and clam base or salt and bring to a boil. Simmer for 15-20 minutes or until the potatoes are done.
4. Add the fish and simmer for 15 minutes.
5. Add the milk, pepper and Tabasco sauce. Bring almost to a boil and serve.

Chapter 8
The Young, the Not So Young and the Special

"Approach love and cooking with reckless abandon"
—*Dalai Lama*

It would be nice and oh so easy if we only had adults to feed but it was not to be, once we completed Centralization of Foodservices for San Diego County. In 1997, we started providing services to the Probation Department that included two Juvenile Halls, two Juvenile Camps and four court mandated school programs. This resulted in a cost savings for Probation while greatly improving their services.

For example, if a child was on a medical diet or was allergic to a food product, they usually gave them a peanut butter and jelly sandwich. Needless to say, their allergy list was quite long as the kids caught on to the fact that if they didn't like the food they could say they were allergic and get a P&J sandwich.

We at the Sheriff had structured diets for all cases and required clarification from a doctor or family member on all allergies. The adult inmates tried the "allergic thing" from anything from oatmeal to peas to spinach. No deal. And these were grown men. Some mothers have called me over the years to tell me their 35 year old acid heads' likes and dislikes. You guessed it; *really* no deal. Therefore, we were ready for the kids and supplied them with balanced diets that fit their allergies.

We now had 9 year old to 18 year old children to feed and keep relatively happy. This was not easy as they were used to fast food and of course that was what they wanted. The problem was that the Juvenile Justice California State regulations and the Federal School Lunch

Program guidelines definitely did not include this type of food. When I was a director in schools, I had the same problem; what can you feed kids that meet regulations and that they would eat? It was difficult to say the least.

It was quite a trick to find a middle road and give the children, (called wards, not inmates), food that they would eat and which fit all the rules. It didn't help matters that some of the wards never had what we call *home cooking* so our roast beef, mashed potatoes and gravy dinner was foreign to them. We wound up putting the beef on a bun with barbecue sauce on it and served it with mashed potatoes and vegetables. We also learned to put condiments, like salad dressing and mayo, on the side. I already knew that they could actually live without split pea soup.

The menu we developed for them ran very close to what we gave the adults; remember I told you that inmates eat pretty much like kids. They all liked the pizza, spaghetti, hamburgers, hot dogs, cookies and cake. We had to leave some things on the menu that was good for them like cereals, vegetables, fresh fruits, salads and eggs. When we served these items with things like a cookie, sandwiches, Jell-O salad, tortillas and beans they were more acceptable. We knew better than to give them creamed *anything* with peas mixed in it or items like corned beef and cabbage.

Occasionally, I would have a parent write me for a recipe because their child said they liked something. One mother wrote me that Junior never had bread pudding before and loved ours so I sent her the recipe. The trick is that we put chocolate chips in it.

We endeavored to provide a Heart Healthy menu with no fried foods, substituting oven baked items with plenty of fresh fruit and vegetables. Hopefully, eating healthy rubbed off on some of them. You never know.

Auden describes home as a place to go out from and come back to. Frost calls it a place that when you have to go there, they have to let you in.

Sadly enough, some of these children actually wind up calling being incarcerated "home". We would see the same kids come back again and again into the Juvenile system, then into one of our medium security jails as an 18 year old adult, into a maximum security jail a year or so later, and eventually disappearing into the State Prison system. They always acted like it was "old home week" and told us why they were with us again and what they were in for this time. It was a hard fact for us to swallow that nothing seemed to help some of them stay straight.

From 1996-2001, we provided foodservices for the Children's Center operated by San Diego County's Health Services. There were children there who ranged from infants to 17 years old. This presented its' own challenges. They too were on the School Breakfast and Lunch Program so those rules had to be met. However, these children were traumatized, sometimes abused children who were separated from their families.

They were allowed all they could eat, as well as food in between meals in their cottages. We still managed to save them money over their old costs as well as provide them with good food. The sad part was some of them eventually wound up in Juvenile Hall.

Mrs. Carmen Cope was the Food Service Supervisor during this time. She had been supervising the women's jail and I told her that going to the Children's Center would be an easier job and give her a little rest from the inmates. (Female inmates are much more difficult to supervise than men) It turned out that this facility, with its' myriad of special needs and problems was far from easier but I think she forgave me. She was absolutely the perfect person for this facility.

When we first started supplying their meals there were 60 children; it went up from there to 245 within a year. It was, after all, rewarding for all of our staff who worked there to provide comfort to these poor kids. What better way than with food? Carmen and her staff had special theme days every week as well as birthday parties and special holiday meals. They all did a fabulous job making the kids and staff happy.

CHOCOLATE CHIP BREAD PUDDING (Serves 8-10)

Since we do not give inmates bread ends, (Heaven forbid), we had to find recipes to use the thousands of bread ends we had each week. So, in addition to bread stuffing, bread crumbs and croutons, we made bread pudding. Since we try to cook "heart healthy" as much as possible, we used a small amount of sugar and relied instead on the sweetness of the pineapple. We made this recipe, minus the chocolate chips, for the jail inmates.

Food Service Supervisor Neila Afan-Cook came up with adding chocolate chips for our Juvenile Wards so they would eat it. Of course, word got out so we had to make it this way for all our jail staff and kitchen inmate workers as well. It was extremely popular! It is also very popular with my family and friends so I make it for almost every occasion and sometimes "just because". There is nothing like a little "jail house" pudding for dessert; simple, inexpensive and delicious. This is a great dish to take to a fancy dinner or pot luck supper. It is beautiful to look at as well as to eat.

Preheat oven to 375 degrees

- 1 ½ loaves French bread or any white day old bread
- 4 ounces (1 stick) melted butter or margarine plus some additional soft butter to grease the pan
- 1 (20 ounce) can crushed pineapple, not drained
- 4 large eggs
- ½ cup granulated sugar
- 3 tablespoons maple syrup
- 1 tablespoon vanilla extract
- 4 cups milk, regular or low fat
- 2 cups mini or 1 cup regular chocolate chips

1. Lightly butter a large baking dish or pan.
2. Cut the bread into cubes and place into pan.
3. Whisk together in a large bowl all ingredients except the chocolate chips.
4. Pour wet mixture over the bread cubes.
5. Put chocolate chips over the top of the mixture and lightly mix it together with your hands. If you wish, you can sprinkle the top with a little granulated sugar.
6. Bake in an oven at 375 degrees for 50-55 minutes until the pudding is set and the top is lightly browned.
7. It is great warm or cold with or without whipped cream.

BANANA STREUSEL MUFFINS (Makes 12 muffins)

We made these addictive muffins in our Juvenile Detention Facilities for the wards and they ate them up with relish. We needed a recipe to use up any overripe bananas and this recipe is perfect. When we had either walnuts and/or raisins available from the School Lunch Program we used them but if not they are still great without them.

Try these for your kids for breakfast along with some yogurt and fruit. We made a terrific Banana Cake with Butter Cream Frosting for the inmates on sheet pans since there was over 6,000 of them. Can you imagine making 6,000 muffins? We couldn't either.

Preheat oven to 375 degrees

Topping:
- 2 ounces (½ stick) butter, cold and cut in cubes
- ½ cup all purpose flour
- ½ cup firmly packed brown sugar
- ½ cup granulated sugar

1. Combine butter, flour, brown sugar and sugar in a bowl.
2. Using a pastry cutter or two forks, mix until soft crumbs are formed. Set aside.

Muffins:

- 2 cups all purpose flour
- 2 teaspoons baking powder
- I teaspoon baking soda
- 2 teaspoons cinnamon
- $\frac{1}{4}$ teaspoon salt
- I large egg
- $\frac{3}{4}$ cup firmly packed brown sugar
- 2 cups ripe mashed bananas
- $\frac{1}{2}$ cup vegetable oil
- $\frac{1}{2}$ cup dairy sour cream
- 2 teaspoons vanilla extract
- $\frac{3}{4}$ cup walnuts, chopped
- $\frac{1}{2}$ cup golden raisins

1. Place paper liners into muffin pans.
2. In a large bowl whisk together flour, baking powder, baking soda, cinnamon and salt. Set aside.
3. In another large bowl whisk together until smooth the egg, brown sugar, bananas, oil, sour cream and vanilla.
4. Stir the flour mixture into the egg mixture with a few light strokes just until the dry ingredients are moistened. (Do not beat!) Stir in the walnuts and raisins.
5. Divide the batter between the paper liners, filling them almost full.
6. Divide the streusel topping among the muffins, placing about 1-2 tablespoons on top of each muffin.
7. Bake at 375 degrees for about 18 minutes or until a toothpick

inserted into the middle of a muffin comes out with a few moist crumbs.

8. Let stand 5 minutes then remove from the pan to a rack to cool.

9. When cool, cover with plastic wrap.

RESTRICTED (SPECIAL) DIETS

We provided restricted medical diets and religious diets; no matter what we did the inmates called them "Special Diets". Some of them like to think they are *very* special. Our Medical Department operated a clinic in every jail and in our four largest jails there were large care units; it was a very sophisticated operation. We had our own renal dialysis clinic in the Central jail and provided dentistry in the jails as well. There were inmates who required all kinds of diets such as diabetic, heart, low sodium/low fat, gastric and dental soft, pregnancy, renal and all kinds of liquid diets. When you throw in every allergy diet known to man, you can see what a challenge this was for the staff.

We had one registered dietician, Ms. Marlene Tutt, who was very patient, knowledgeable and hard working. I received this position after begging for one for 14 years. Up to that time, I did most of the diet consults myself which was really fun! When we started doing our own renal dialysis, they saw the wisdom of giving me this position. I thanked God every day for Ms. Tutt who is still there and working hard to provide quality nutritional services to the inmates.

We fed thousands each day and at least 10 percent of them were diets. On top of that, these inmates flowed in and out of jail and were constantly changing. For instance, one of our challenges was we had "not so young" inmates, up to 104 years old. There was a 98 year old man in for the mercy killing of his wife. Within a few days he was joined by a 103 year old man in for aggravated assault with intent to commit great bodily harm. (What stamina he must have had) They required special evaluation and a specific diet was written for each of them.

There were some other interesting diets. We had a man with no arms, arrested for "armed robbery". He was in a wheelchair and he actually held and shot a gun with his *feet*! (I would have liked to have been a fly on the wall at his court hearing; a man with no arms committing "armed robbery"!) He also *ate* with his feet and thus became someone we needed to evaluate. Ms. Tutt, our dietician, observed him during a meal time to ascertain if he actually could get enough food into his mouth. He did fine as he was used to this method of eating although it was quite messy and not pretty to watch.

Another inmate kept requesting a "soft diet". Since this order was not coming from our Medical staff, I went to see him. It seems he had no teeth; he said "we" had lost them when we transferred him from one jail to another. (I gave up trying to find out why the teeth weren't in his mouth during the transfer)

He had been in jail long enough to know that if he went to Medical they would order him put on a blended liquid diet and he hated it. He said his gums were really tough and could handle a dental soft. I love it when the inmates do the thinking for us so I took his word for it and granted him his wish.

We had a female prostitute that was a real piece of work; she was also diabetic. She manipulated her disease to get what she wanted such as a different housing unit or roommates. She would buy a lot of commissary food items and put herself in a comma if she didn't get her way. I had a talk with her and tried to explain to her how she should be eating to control her disease so it wouldn't cause her body so much damage.

She didn't listen. She played around one too many times and accidentally died in her cell one day. We really hate it when someone dies while incarcerated and we try everything we can to see that things like this do not happen.

In addition, we provided all established Religious diets, such as Kosher and Muslim, to the best of our ability. Please see Chapter 7 for some of our favorite ones.

We had many inmates come in with most diseases known to man such as Aids or HIV, or just severely emaciated due to taking drugs or using alcohol. If you would like a good reason to Not to take drugs, come in sometime and look at some of the 30 year olds with almost no liver or kidney function; that should cure you.

We would put them on a high protein diet along with a boosted shake or a can of Ensure twice a day. In addition, we had a lot of wired jaw diets for various reasons and we made this shake part of the "blended diet". It made the diet more palatable since the balance of this diet is regular food put through a blender. Just picture a drink of spaghetti and meatballs or chili and vegetables and you'll see what I mean. The milk shake also helped to provide much needed nutrients and calories.

BOOSTED MILKSHAKE

Try this shake if you have someone recuperating from an illness or an elderly person who needs some protein and calories in their diet but are usually too tired to eat a lot. It really helps them nutritionally in a delicious way.

Mix a banana, 4 ounces fruit juice, 1 can of Ensure, 1 cup fresh or canned fruit and ½ cup vanilla ice cream in a blender. Serve cold.

ORANGE GLAZED CHICKEN (Serves 6)

I developed this chicken recipe while working in hospitals to fit most of the diets. It tastes delicious and goes well with any kind of rice, mashed potatoes or couscous. We started using this dish for our diets in jail and then expanded it to the inmates and staff as well where it fast became a favorite.

*Note: there are a few variations of this dish. You can use skinless, boneless chicken; just cook it for a shorter time. Also, you can use a whole, 4-5 pound chicken; the cooking temperature would be 415 degrees. Pour 1/3 of the orange mixture over the chicken and roast for 30 minutes. Remove the chicken and turn it over on its' breast. Pour 1/3 of the mixture over the chicken. Return the chicken to the oven and roast for 30 minutes. Remove the chicken and flip it back over, pour the remaining mixture over the chicken and roast for 30 minutes longer. Test the chicken to assure that it is done.

You can put all kinds of fresh herbs, such as parsley, basil or rosemary, in the cavity and under the breast skin of the chicken to give it extra flavor. This chicken is great either way you do it, so crispy and golden on the outside and tender on the inside. No one has to be the wiser that it is actually good for you as well.

Preheat oven to 375 degrees

- 6 pieces chicken quarters (legs and thighs or breast and wing)
- Salt and pepper
- 12 ounces orange juice concentrate
- 1 tablespoon cinnamon
- 1 teaspoon nutmeg
- 1 tablespoon crushed garlic

1. Sprinkle chicken pieces lightly with salt and pepper.

2. Place in a tin foil lined baking pan (it will be a lot easier to clean later)

3. Mix together the orange juice concentrate, cinnamon, nutmeg and garlic.

4. Spoon half the mixture over the chicken.

5. Bake the chicken for 30 minutes at 375 degrees.

6. Spoon the other half of the mixture over the chicken. Cook for 20 minutes longer or until the chicken is cooked through and the skin is golden and crispy. Serve with the cooking juices.

DISCIPLINARY ISOLATION DIET
(quoted from the California State, Title 15 Regulations)

This diet is served to inmates to help control their behavior. One half of this meat loaf is served twice a day with 2 slices of whole wheat bread and water. The recipe is actually in Title 15 which is the California State regulations. There are strict rules in the use of this diet and it must be ordered by the Facility Administrator and used only for a specified amount of time.

When I first went behind bars and heard about the "loaf", I thought it was absolutely the most ridiculous thing I ever heard of until I saw that it actually worked. It works on male inmates but the female inmates normally could care less. It worked very well on *all* the inmates in San Diego as we had good food and the inmates missed it. The meat loaf is actually good; the only thing missing is catsup.

One day I thought that the jail commanders should taste the diet so they would know what they were ordering. Therefore, I brought it to a Command Staff Meeting along with the whole wheat bread. They were only supposed to taste it but they ate every bit of it and loved it. They made sandwiches and had a good time. They were surprised that it was so good and still worked; I think it is just the *idea* of it.

Other states have various forms of this diet as well, some of which are not as good as ours. Some inmates even take it to court. For example, in one state there was an inmate named "John". He was incarcerated for slitting a man's throat. When he got to prison he attacked the prison guards and other inmates with sharpened poles, feces and homemade weapons. He was put on the Disciplinary diet.

John argued that the "nutraloaf" was cruel and unusual punishment and violated his 8th Amendment rights. He really knows about violating other people's rights, yes? In the end, he did not win. (Poor baby) Morale of the story; be good when you go to jail, unless the regular food stinks and the loaf would be a welcome change.

Preheat oven to 350 degrees

- 2 ½ ounces nonfat dry milk
- 4 ½ ounces raw grated potato
- 3 ounces raw carrots, chopped or grated fine
- 1 ½ ounces tomato juice or puree
- 4 ½ ounces raw cabbage, grated fine
- 7 ounces lean ground beef, turkey or Textured Vegetable Protein (TVP)
- 2 ½ ounces oil
- 1 ½ ounces whole wheat flour
- ¼ teaspoon salt
- 4 teaspoons raw onion, chopped
- 1 large egg
- 4 teaspoons chili powder
- 6 ounces dry red beans, precooked

1. Shape all ingredients into a loaf and bake at 350-375 degrees for 50-70 minutes.

*Note: We baked the loaf at 350 degrees for 60 minutes. They give you a big range here, why I don't know. Maybe it compensates for those people who have ovens that do not work properly; we made sure our ovens worked just fine.

❧❧

Holiday meals were also provided to the inmates. We always did a full Thanksgiving dinner, complete with Roast Turkey, stuffing, mashed potatoes, turkey gravy, cranberry sauce, vegetables, chef's salad with dressing, hot rolls and butter and of course pumpkin pie.

We went all out for Christmas as well. They had roast beef and gravy, oven roasted potatoes, vegetables, chef's salad with dressing, rolls and butter, Christmas layer cake and Christmas candy. New Year's was always celebrated with a ham dinner with candied yams and black eyed peas for good luck for the year. (For the inmates, it could only get better)

We also honored Passover; we allowed a rabbi to come in and bring some traditional food for the Jewish inmates to eat during the ceremony.

We had a Muslim diet and during Ramadan, a month of self-reflecting and fasting, we served them one meal a day after dark. We usually started out with dozens of inmates but when some of them found out that they were expected to fast all day, they dropped out. I guess they were new to the religion. The devout Muslim inmates observed the entire month.

In addition, we did some special menus like something barbequed on the Fourth of July and our famous Ugly Duckling cake on Easter. I think our extra efforts were appreciated by most of the inmates as we received many complimentary written and verbal comments from them. It doesn't hurt to be nice when you can, yes?

Chapter 9

Cooking with Conviction

Comfort me with apples for I am sick of love.
—*The Bible*

There are many, many programs for inmates in jails and prisons to offer them assistance in becoming more viable members of our society when they are released from custody. We in corrections work very hard to assure that the inmates do not become repeat customers. There are AA and NA programs to help inmates with their addictions, many training programs to teach them new work skills such as landscaping, farming and printing, educational programs such as the GED program and of course training in all aspects of food service.

At the Women's Community Correctional Center in Kailua, Hawaii, instructors from Kapi'olani Community College teach 10-20 women a course called Fundamentals of Cooking. Over the 14 week course, the inmates receive instruction in all aspects of cooking; they serve the fruits of their labor to the appreciative staff. The instructors had to get used to the knives attached to metal cords to the main table as well as keeping the proper distance between themselves and their students. Other than that, they said that it was much like teaching in college except at times it was much more rewarding.

The classes are meant to give the inmates cooking skills and more importantly to inspire them to new careers when they are released. To quote one female inmate, "We are all good people; we just made some wrong choices. If you believe in yourself, anything is possible." I guess this course is accomplishing its goals.

Food Service offers many programs such as teaching inmates to clean, cook and bake. For years in San Diego, we have operated a program to teach inmates about food safety and sanitation. They attend classes for 8 weeks, taught by an excellent instructor, Mr. Matt Russo, through the local school district. It covers a multitude of subjects including food safety, bio-hazards, common food borne illnesses, health and hygiene and pest control. They work in the kitchen at the same time, learning to apply what they learn in actual hands on instruction.

At the end of the class, they are given an exam and if they pass with a high enough grade they receive a Food Safety Manager Certificate. Since every food service establishment in California, as well as other states, is required to have at least one person with this certificate working on the premises, this gives an edge to the inmate when he/she is applying for work after their release.

Every year, at least 180 inmates receive their certification certificates in addition to over 600 Grossmont High School certificates and 600 food handler cards. You should see how happy they are when they are presented their certificates in a ceremony. Since many of them have not graduated from school, this gives them the self confidence to move ahead when they leave the facility and hopefully it will help them not to come back.

In addition, all kinds of religious programs are offered to them to both continue their religious practices as well as help them find God. Many criminologists believe that the best hope for an inmate to avoid being incarcerated again is to undergo a religious conversion experience while inside the institution. For many of them, they have hit rock bottom and finding religion literally saves their lives.

Kairos is a Christian prison ministry that operates in many prisons throughout the U.S. Kairos started in California in 1985 and is still going strong today. They hold a three day retreat in the prison chapel for one yard at a time where a course is offered by an interdenominational team.

The volunteers come in and cook for them offering them meals during the retreat that they would not normally get in the prison. Many of the inmates assist in this function and are taught food service skills during this time. In the beginning, the food is a big draw but the inmates wind up getting a lot more out of the experience. One of the results is many of the inmates who attend these retreats do not come back to prison.

Karios also offers a retreat for women on the outside of the facilities in various churches; not only x-inmates attend but also any women who are wives, girlfriends, mothers and relatives of the inmates are eligible to attend as well.

Ms Joan Faustman, a retired San Diego Sheriff Food Service Supervisor, is one of the volunteers for both programs. She spoke to me about how wonderful it makes her feel to be able to help people to develop pride in themselves by achieving pride in their work. These volunteers sometimes feel that they get a lot more out of the experience than they give; to the inmates they are literally their saviors. Everybody wins.

Karios has graciously allowed me to share these recipes, which are made in their prison program, with you. I hope you enjoy them as much as I do.

SENSATIONAL SOUTH AFRICAN RICE SALAD
(Serves 6)

This is a great salad and good for you too! I used apples which are crunchy and went well in the salad. You can add shrimp or scallops or crab as well. I also served it along side cold sliced roast lamb, roast beef or turkey. It was great even the next day.

I brought this salad to a pot luck for one of the organizations I belong to; Les Dames d' Escoffier. I was a bit hesitant because all these fabulous Chefs and Cook Book Writers had brought their food as well but my salad was well liked and appreciated. I told them much later that it was from a Prison cooking program.

- 1 ½ cups long grained brown rice, cooked and cooled
- 1 ½ cups chopped fresh peaches or apples
- 1 cup chopped celery
- ¼ cup each chopped green pepper and green onions
- ¼ cup sunflower seeds
- ¼ cup chopped raisins
- 6 ounces frozen baby peas
- 1 handful bean sprouts

Dressing:
- ¼ cup olive oil
- ¼ cup safflower oil (can use any vegetable oil)
- 1 tablespoon lemon juice
- 1 ½ tablespoons chopped parsley
- ½ tablespoon honey
- ½ tablespoon curry powder
- ½ tablespoon soy sauce
- Herb salt to taste

1. Place all the salad ingredients in a large bowl.
2. Shake all dressing ingredients together until mixed.
3. Add the dressing to the salad ingredients and mix well just before serving.

LAZY ME CAKE (Serves 6-8)

How easy do you want it? Your family will think you are a wizard in the kitchen when you whip this up for dinner, even after working all day. This cake is not only easy but delicious; it could become addictive!

Variation: I used only one can of apple pie filling plus: three apples, chopped in pieces, skin on, that I sautéed in two tablespoons of butter. You can also double the sautéed apples and not use canned apple pie filling at all. This recipe works well with canned cherry pie filling as well.

Of course, you must serve it warm with Vanilla Bean Ice Cream. This cake was so good that I couldn't stop tasting it before bringing it to a luncheon to serve. Thank goodness it was a relative who knows that I am a "taster" when I can get away with it.

Preheat oven to 350 degrees

- 2 cans (22 ounces each) apple pie filling
- I box yellow cake mix
- 6 ounces chopped walnuts
- 2 sticks margarine, melted

1. Layer apples evenly on the bottom of a 9x12 pan. Sprinkle dry cake mix over apples.
2. Spread walnuts on top. Drizzle melted margarine over all.
3. Bake at 350 degrees for 45 minutes.

POTATO CHIP COOKIES (Makes 3 dozen cookies)

Note: Watch these cookies closely as they will burn; mine took barely 12 minutes. They are light and lacy and Oh So Good! I tried them with butter instead of margarine because usually everything is "better with butter". However, they were a little too rich that way so I went back to margarine. I made this recipe several times until I ran out of potato chips and I don't even eat potato chips. The things I do for my readers.

I bring these cookies to sick friends, pot luck suppers and as a thank you for services rendered. They are always a hit and no one has yet to guess they are made with potato chips. They all think that they have white chocolate or macadamia nuts in them. They could really call them "Surprise Cookies".

Preheat oven to 350 degrees

- 2 sticks (8ounces) margarine, softened
- I teaspoon vanilla
- ¾ cup sugar
- 1¾ cup flour
- ¾ cup crushed potato chips

1. In an electric mixer, blend together margarine, vanilla and sugar; cream well.
2. Blend in the flour and then the potato chips. (dough will be firm)
3. Drop by teaspoonfuls onto ungreased cookie sheet.
4. Bake in 350 degree oven for 12-15 minutes

Chapter 10

New Orleans

Let the Good Times Roll
(Laissez Les Bons Temps Rouler)

NEW ORLEANS PARRISH SHERIFF, LOUISANNA

New Orleans gets a separate chapter for the mere fact they *are special* in so many ways. Major Jim Beach is the Food Service Director for the New Orleans Parrish Sheriff. I was their food service consultant to design and build a 60,000 square foot Central Kitchen; it turned out to be a really beautiful facility. New Orleans had over 7,000 inmates and 2,000 staff in 12 jails, within walking distance of each other. Jim and his staff were responsible for providing three meals a day to everyone out of the Central Kitchen which in itself was a huge task.

On August 29, 2005, a category 5 hurricane named Katrina hit New Orleans with sustained 140 mph winds causing unheard of devastation. An hours' worth of its storm winds is the equivalent to the force *of 5 atomic bombs,* the size dropped on Hiroshima. This is a story of what happened during Hurricane Katrina as told to me by Major Beach. It is an inspiring, graphic example of what some foodservice people in corrections go through in the course of doing their duty to the best of their ability.

Jim was notified on August 28th that the storm was headed for New Orleans. They did what they always do; they went into a two day hurricane drill. All the food service personnel reported to the kitchen, prepared to stay for two days. Most of them brought their families with them. It is like a big picnic where the families get together and cook and play video games and then go home.

This time it was different; it wasn't a drill but the real thing. By the morning of the 29th, part of the kitchen's roof was blown off so the families were evacuated to the Community Correctional Center Jail behind the kitchen. The food service staff continued to work, preparing meals and shipping them out to the jails. The radios and power had failed and they were on generators.

By early morning of the 30th, the storm had stopped but the flooding grew worse. What no one knew yet was that the city's levee system was disintegrating. Water was pouring into the city at a rate of millions of gallons a minute. The generators failed and all communication in the city was gone. The staff continued to wade and swim in 5 feet of water from the kitchen to the closest jail, carrying as much food and water as they could. The water was contaminated with diesel fuel, raw sewage, rats and garbage.

There was water everywhere and the flooding continued; each jail was an island unto itself with each warden trying to handle the problems with the inmates as well as dealing with the staff and 500 civilians, including women, children and pets.

With food and water on half rations and every one trying to sleep in the dark on concrete floors in 100 degree heat, the mood was dismal. The inmates started to break up the jails as well as trying to break the windows to get air. There was rioting and fires were started. The staff was in despair as they knew there was little hope for their homes and people left behind as 80% (2100 square miles) of New Orleans was under water. Jim had to post guards to secure the food and water as well as protect the civilians from inmates if they should escape.

The Food Service Staff kept to their posts, doing what they could to help everyone survive. I teased Jim that I pictured them with a gun in one hand and a spatula in the other. They worked with little sleep under actual fear of death and endured the hardship without complaint, never leaving their stations. This was a true testament to Jim's leadership abilities as well as the staff's training and integrity.

For the next three days, with three small boats that the Sheriff commandeered, they started evacuating the inmates to the highest point in the city, the Broad Street Overpass Bridge. They secured and guarded the inmates on the bridge until finally helicopters and busses were sent to evacuate everyone to jails and prisons away from the flood. Jim and his staff assisted in this task and they were among the last to be evacuated; it was 5 days of pure hell!

This experience was extremely hard on everyone and changed many of their lives. 90% of them lost their homes and belongings in the flood. It was a miracle that no one was killed in the jails as at least 1700 people were killed by Katrina. They also lost their Central Kitchen to the flood but they are in the process of rebuilding it, bigger and better than before.

Major Jim Beach was an ordinary person who performed heroically during extraordinary times. He was awarded the Food Service Industry's highest honor; the Silver Plate Award in 2010. Very few people in Corrections receive this honor and no one deserved it more.

TILAPIA JAMBALAYA (Serves 6-8 people)
Submitted by Major Jim Beach

Jambalaya is a traditional Louisiana dish that is loved by everyone, including the inmates. It was made with just sausage until thousands of pounds of Tilapia was made available to the jails at a cheap cost. In order to use the fish, they decreased the amount of sausage in the original recipe and added the Tilapia. I had never seen a recipe for this dish until the jail made it. It is quite good; the fish cooks up nicely in the Jambalaya and has the texture of shrimp. They serve it with mustard greens and bread. (Remember to cook the death out of the greens) You can add a little heat by adding 2 teaspoons cayenne pepper or hot sauce to the recipe.

*Note: To give you an example of what I had to do with most of the recipes I received, here is part of the original recipe that fed <u>6,300 people.</u>

- 8 gal oil
- 1,050 pounds onions
- 1,656 pounds celery
- 1,728 pounds green peppers
- 450 pounds rice
- 675 pounds smoked turkey sausage
- 900 pounds tilapia

Can you imagine all this food in one spot? We are talking literally about <u>tons</u> of food! They do it all day long in jails. It is no wonder that most of us jail food service employees have trouble functioning in a small kitchen with *baby* equipment when we go home.

- 3 tablespoons vegetable oil
- 1 medium onion, chopped
- 1 yellow or green pepper, chopped
- 2 stalks celery, chopped
- 2 teaspoons garlic powder
- 1 can (28 ounces) diced tomatoes, not drained
- 2 bay leaves
- 3 cups chicken broth
- 2 cups raw white rice
- 3 cups smoked turkey sausage, cut in pieces
- 2 teaspoons salt
- 1 tablespoon black pepper
- 1 # raw tilapia, cut in 1" pieces

1. Heat the oil in a Dutch oven. Add the onion, peppers, celery and garlic powder. Sauté until light brown, stirring occasionally.

2. Add tomatoes and bay leaves, cook 5 minutes. Add chicken broth and rice; cook for 10 minutes.
3. Add the sausage, salt and pepper; cover and cook for 15-20 minutes or until the rice is tender.
4. Add the tilapia and cook for 5-10 minutes, stirring occasionally.

RED BEANS WITH SAUSAGE (Serves 6-8)

This dish is served in jail over rice with turnip greens and bread. It is another favorite with the inmates which is a good thing since they get it quite often. It is filling and delicious. Since they are cooking for 8-9,000 people, they keep it mild but you can add some Tabasco sauce if you like it hot.

- ½ pound small red beans (soak overnight in water and then drain)
- 2 cups smoked chicken sausage
- 1 large onion, chopped
- 3 stalks celery, chopped
- 1 green pepper, chopped
- 2 tablespoons garlic powder
- 1 teaspoon salt
- 2 bay leaves
- 1 tablespoon onion flakes
- Water
- 1 tablespoon black pepper

1. Place the drained beans in a Dutch oven or heavy kettle. Add the sausage, onion, celery, green pepper, garlic powder, salt, bay leaves and onion flakes.

2. Add enough water to cover the beans. Bring to a boil and then simmer, uncovered for 2 hours. Be careful that the beans do not dry out or stick; you may have to add a little more water.

3. Add the pepper and continue cooking, covered, with the heat low, for 1 more hour. Correct the seasonings. You may have to add a bit more salt and/or pepper.

Just in case you go to Mardi Gras someday and wind up in jail, this is a sample daily menu for a New Orleans jail.

Breakfast: Applesauce, 2 ounces cheese tidbits, buttered grits and milk.

Lunch: Red beans and sausage, steamed rice, turnip greens, 2 slices of bread and fruit punch.

Dinner: Two chicken bologna sandwiches, purple plums and fruit punch.

Chapter 11

Down South

Are You Keeping Sweet?
—*Old Southern Expression*

I really love the South, its' people, slow ways, gentle smiles and wonderful food! Yes, a lot of it is lard, which makes the most tender pie crust you ever had, fatback and ham hocks that flavor the vegetables and all the fried morsels that sing in your mouth. I am a big believer in enjoying all we can while we are able but keep it in moderation.

The jails, like the area, have good food but the facilities are sometimes not the best and there *are* those chain gangs. I guess you have to take the good with the bad; the food helps a lot. "Are you keeping sweet?" really says it all about this corner of our country.

MISSISSIPPI

CHICKEN GIZZARD STEW (Serves 4-6)

The original jail recipe said to put the gizzards in a steam kettle and cook for a while until they are soft. Then throw in all your *squishy* vegetables like peppers, tomatoes, squash and cabbage with some salt and pepper and cook it some more.

We in Corrections work with a limited budget and have been known to use all of our leftovers in inventive ways. It took a few phone calls to the recipe submitter as well as making a few batches of stew to get this right. He and I agreed you *do not* have to wait for the vegetables to get squishy; you can basically use anything, even *fresh* vegetables. I could tell that this was a new thought process for him. I assure you it is just as good.

I freeze individual servings in pint size zip lock bags so I can enjoy this stew for a longer time. Since I could not get any of my regular tasters except one to taste it, I had to do <u>something</u> with it. I told them that chicken gizzards, in a stew or soup as well as in gravy with rice or mashed potatoes, are served regularly throughout the South. They said to get some *Southern* tasters. I finally got some people to taste it and they loved it. Moral of the story; do not tell anyone *before* they eat it there are "chicken gizzards" in it, just say it's chicken.

*Note: I use a pressure cooker in this recipe because it takes quite a while for the gizzards to get tender in a regular pot. If you do not have a pressure cooker you can use a heavy soup pot; it will just take more time. Add the second batch of vegetables when the gizzards are fork tender. This stew is delicious and is well worth the time. This can be served by itself or over noodles or rice.

- 2 tablespoons vegetable oil
- ¼ onion, chopped
- 5 stalks celery, chopped
- 1-1 ½ pounds chicken gizzards
- 1 pound parsnips, cubed
- 1 red pepper, cubed
- ½ bok choy, chopped or ¼ head cabbage
- 1 can (14.5 ounces) chopped tomatoes
- 32 ounces chicken broth
- 2 medium yellow squash, sliced
- 1 medium zucchini, sliced
- 2 tablespoons fresh parsley, chopped
- 6 plum tomatoes, chopped
- Salt and pepper to taste

1. Heat the vegetable oil in a pressure cooker.

2. Sauté the onion and 2 stalks of celery until lightly brown over medium heat. Add the chicken gizzards and cook for about 5 minutes, stirring occasionally.

3. Add 3 stalks of celery, parsnips, red pepper, bok choy, canned tomatoes and chicken broth. Put the lid and the top on the pressure cooker. Cook over medium heat until the top starts shaking; turn the heat to simmer. The top should be rocking gently. Cook for 30 minutes.

4. Turn off the heat and let sit 5 minutes. Set pot in sink and slowly run cool water over lid until the steam vent closes and you can remove the top and the lid.

5. Return to heat. Add the yellow squash, zucchini, parsley and tomatoes. Cook over medium heat, uncovered, until the vegetables are soft; season to taste with salt and pepper.

We waste nothing in jail so what to do with those leftover grits? Now you can make Fried Grits, like folks do in Mississippi jails, which some people think taste better than normal grits. You can serve them in place of polenta, potatoes or rice. If you have any cornmeal mush leftover, that will work here as well. This was a helpful suggestion from the jail cook in Mississippi.

I personally never even *have* cornmeal mush in the first place. It is not my thing. It was on the menu when I started in San Diego. The main complaint was that the inmates were flushing it down the toilet and clogging the system. It came off the menu because I wouldn't eat it myself. I hear they <u>do</u> eat it in the South.

To make fried grits, just chill your leftover grits in a flat pan, cut them into pieces, dip them in flour, fry in hot oil and of course sprinkle with salt. *Note: kids like this recipe; it is fried, right?

ALABAMA

These recipes from Alabama were submitted by Barbara Holly, Food Service Manager for the State of Alabama, now retired. Barbara is a Silver Plate Winner, as well as many other awards, and is highly regarded in our industry. She was a favorite of the inmates under her care as well even if most of them did not know her name.

AUNT JACK'S AWESOME BROWNIES
(Submitted by a retired female warden of a women's prison)

These are delicious, sinfully sweet brownies. I made half with pecans and half without to please some of my family. Serve them with ice cream to compliment their rich flavor and of course a big glass of milk.

*Note: the cake batter is like soft dough. You will need to pat it out in the bottom of the pan. When you add the other half of the mix on the top, drop it in lumps as close together as possible; it will spread out as it bakes.

Preheat oven to 350 degrees

- 1 box German chocolate cake mix
- 1 stick (4 ounces) butter (the real thing, not margarine)
- 2/3 cup evaporated milk (like Pet or Carnation)
- 6 ounces semi-sweet chocolate chips (the real kind)
- 14 ounces Kraft caramels (no low fat ones, old fashioned ones only)
- 2 cups pecans, finely chopped

1. Combine the cake mix, butter, 1/3 cup evaporated milk and 1 cup pecans in a bowl and mix until soft.
2. Put half of the mix into a greased 13x9 pan and bake at 350 degrees for 6 minutes. (Aunt Jack insists that this is the perfect time)
3. Melt the caramels with 1/3 cup evaporated milk in a double boiler.
4. Sprinkle the chocolate chips over the cake mixture in the pan.
5. Pour the caramel on top of the chips and sprinkle the remaining pecans on top of that.
6. Put the remaining cake mix on top of the mixture and bake at 350 degrees for 12-15 minutes.
7. Cool and cut into squares. Enjoy!

COUNTRY COLLARD GREENS AND HAM HOCKS (Serves 4-6)

*Mess—any measured amount of fresh vegetables necessary to serve a given amount of people.

When I received the original recipe from Barbara it didn't say what a "mess" was so I asked her, even though I had a rough idea. She gave me the above answer. I used 3 pounds of collards for this recipe. The collards in my store are sold in bunches tied together and they weigh approximately 1 pound per bunch. An easy way to cut the collards is to wash them and then lay the bunch down flat, roll them into a loose long roll and cut them into wedges. This is a great way to get your vitamins!

You must serve these collards with cornbread as no self respecting Southerner would eat them without it. You need to soak up the "pot liquor" or pan juice and it is best done with cornbread.

- 1 ½ pounds fresh ham hocks
- 1 tablespoon vegetable oil
- 1 * mess (3#) fresh collard greens
- 2 cups water
- Salt and pepper to taste
- 1 tablespoon cane syrup (Karo)

1. Brown ham hocks in a large skillet with 1 tablespoon vegetable oil.
2. Wash collard greens; cut them in large pieces.
3. Place the greens and the water on top of the ham hocks.
4. Cover and cook over medium low heat for about an hour or until the greens are tender. (add a little more water if necessary)
5. Add the salt, pepper and syrup; cover and cook another 15 minutes.
6. Pull the meat out of the hocks and break into small pieces. Add the meat to the greens and serve with vinegar on the side.

CRANBERRY RELISH (Serves 10)

This relish goes with everything; pork chops, fried chicken and even meatloaf. Kids love it!

- 1 ¼ cups boiling water
- 6 ounce package strawberry Jell-o
- 1 can whole cranberry sauce
- 8 ounce can crushed pineapple, not drained
- ¼ cup orange juice
- 1 cup pecans, chopped

1. Dissolve Jell-o in boiling water.
2. Add cranberry sauce and stir until mixed well.
3. Add all other ingredients and mix well.
4. Refrigerate until firm.

SOUTHERN STYLE CHICKEN AND DRESSING
(Serves 6)

Casserole dishes are used a lot in jails as they are easy, quick and filling. This dish is delicious and oh so Southern. Serve it with the cranberry relish and green beans. Make sure you cook the green beans the Southern way; that is to say to "death" and add some fat back or bacon. In California they would be green and "ala dente" but not taste half so good.

- 1 fat hen (4-5 pounds)
- 1 cup onions, chopped
- 1 cup celery, chopped
- ½ cup butter
- 5-6 cups cornbread, crumbled
- ½ loaf day old bread or rolls
- 4 large eggs
- 3 cups chicken broth
- 1 tablespoon baking powder
- 1 tablespoon salt
- 1 tablespoon pepper
- 1 tablespoon dry sage
- 1 can (10 ounces) cream of chicken soup

1. Boil the hen until it is done. Remove the hen from the broth,

cool and debone it, cutting the chicken into pieces. Reserve the broth.

2. Sauté the onions and celery in the butter until light brown.
3. Crumble the cornbread and bread in a large baking dish. Add the onion mixture and mix it well with your hands.
4. Mix all of the rest of the ingredients together; pour over the cornbread mixture. Mix well with your hands.
5. Add the chicken pieces and mix them into the bread mixture.
6. Bake in a 350 degree oven for 35-45 minutes or until set and brown.
7. Serve with chicken gravy.

*Note: This makes a good pot luck dish; just bring a good amount of chicken gravy on the side as it has a tendency to dry out on you.

Sample Daily Menu in Alabama:
   Breakfast: Orange drink, grits, scrambled eggs, biscuits and gravy and milk.
   Lunch: Tuna salad, French fries, corn, tangy spinach, hot buttered rolls, bread pudding with lemon sauce.
   Dinner: Chicken and rice, northern beans, fresh cabbage, buttered cornbread, stewed apple, lemon drink.

VIRGINIA

TOMATO ASPIC SALAD (Serves 6)

This recipe is *almost* exactly like the one served in a Virginian jail. The recipe is from a job I had with a department store chain in Virginia and it was top secret for years. Naturally, it has a story to it. That is why it has stuck in my mind for over 30 years.

I was the manager for the store's quite extensive food service. All the cooking staff had been working there for almost all their lives. They were always very civil to me but almost never talked to me as I was an outsider from the North and a woman manager to boot. There were very few women managing food services in those days.

One day the head cook came and told me that "Zoe" was going on vacation for two weeks and for that time, we would not have tomato aspic salad on the menu. It seems that she had been making it for 30 years and no one else had the recipe. This didn't make sense to me; you have to forgive me, I was kind of new there. So...... I went to speak to her.

She told me that no one else had ever had to make it. I wasn't getting anywhere with her so I asked her what we would do if the "Good Lord took her today" and no one knew how to make it? Wouldn't she like it to be made after she was gone as well? She thought about it and said I was right and that she would teach someone that day before she left.

Early the next morning, my head cook called and was very upset. She said, "Zoe had done passed". I asked, "Passed where?" She said, "Passed over to the Lord, just like you told her she was going to do". She had died from a heart attack just before midnight! She was only in her forties. I felt so bad; what a poor example I chose to give her.

I went to the funeral and no one would sit near me. They thought that I was a witch and could tell the future. However, from that time until I left, everyone did everything I said without complaint. Believe me, I have not told anyone else they might die even though it may have made some of my jobs a lot easier to take.

*Note: In jail, they sometimes add canned fruit (drained) to the mixture as well as other chopped vegetables such as cabbage. They don't get the fancy presentation though; it is usually just placed in the serving tray. You will find Jell-o salads of some sort in jails everywhere, all over the world.

- 4 cups tomato juice
- ½ cup pureed tomatoes
- ½ cup onions, chopped
- ½ cup green peppers, chopped
- 2 stalks celery, chopped
- 3 teaspoons sugar
- 2 tablespoons fresh lemon juice
- 1 tablespoon chopped parsley
- 1 teaspoon salt
- 1 teaspoon black pepper
- ½ teaspoon Tabasco sauce
- 4 ½ teaspoons unflavored gelatin
- ½ cup cold water
- 1 cup carrots, finely grated
- (You can also add crabmeat, avocado or other vegetables)

1. Mix the tomato juice, tomatoes, onions, green peppers, celery, sugar, lemon juice, parsley, salt, pepper and tobacco sauce in a medium sauce pan. Bring to a boil and simmer for 30 minutes.
2. Sprinkle the gelatin over the cold water and mix; let stand 5 minutes to soften.
3. Mix the tomato mixture with the gelatin. Rinse a 6-8 cup mold with water and shake out the excess water. Pour the tomato mixture into the mold.
4. Chill in the refrigerator until the mixture is half set. Add the carrots.
5. Return the salad to the refrigerator until completely chilled and set.
6. Cut into slices and serve on lettuce leaves with a small dollop of mayo on top.

LEMON CHESS PIE (Serves 6)

This is a not too sweet, very pleasing and lemony pie that has been made for *centuries* in Virginia. This pie dates back to 1440. It originally had cheese in it; the word *chess* is a corruption of the word cheese. The cheese has now been replaced with lemon.

In jail they roll the pie dough out onto 18x26 sheet pans and then pour the filling on top. It is baked, chilled and then cut into 54 squares and served as a special treat. It is not usually stolen by the kitchen inmate workers because it doesn't do well when put in your pants although it has been tried. (Inmate clothing have no pockets so everything they steal goes in their pants)

Preheat oven to 350 degrees

- 1 pie crust, 9" uncooked (You can use the English pie crust in Chapter 1 or your own)
- 6 large eggs
- ½ cup sugar
- 1 tablespoon all purpose flour
- 1 tablespoon cornmeal
- 2 tablespoons unsalted butter, softened
- ¼ cup fresh lemon juice
- 3 teaspoons lemon peel, finely grated

1. Beat the eggs with the sugar until light and fluffy.
2. Add the flour, cornmeal, butter, juice and lemon peel and mix well.
3. Pour the mixture into the pie shell, making sure you prick the bottom of the crust first.
4. Bake at 350 degrees for 45 minutes or until the filling is set. Cool before slicing.

CREAM OF PEANUT SOUP (Serves 6)

This is another old recipe, well known in Virginia. In the jail, they use the base they make for their chicken soup that has the broth and pieces of onion, celery and carrot in it. Instead of half and half, they use reconstituted non fat dry milk, both to cut down on the fat and the cost. Of course, there is no garnish. In most restaurants, they strain out the cooked vegetables before adding the peanut butter and half and half to give it that satiny look. I like it with the vegetables like they make it in jail myself; you can try it both ways and see which one you like. This is one of those recipes that are definitely not seen in the Northern or the Western jails; poor babies!

- ¼ cup margarine or butter
- I medium onion, minced
- 2 stalks of celery, minced
- 3 tablespoons flour
- 8 cups chicken broth
- 2 cups peanut butter, smooth preferred
- I ¾ cups half and half

1. In a large soup pot, melt the margarine and sauté the onions and celery until lightly browned.
2. Stir in the flour and cook for 2-3 minutes, stirring constantly.
3. Add the chicken broth and bring to a boil; reduce the heat and cook, stirring often for 15 minutes.
4. With a wire whip, blend in the peanut butter and half and half over low heat until creamy. Do not boil.
5. Serve garnished with chopped peanuts if desired.

FLORIDA

ALLIGATOR STEW (Serves 6-8)

In Florida they sometimes have to thin out the alligator population so the jails get some alligator meat for free. They then make alligator stew and the inmates love it. They also grind it, add some seasonings and make burgers with it which they love as well.

People here in California pay lots of money for those burgers in restaurants as it is something different. It is a very mild meat so it needs some spice to zip it up. Try it for your family for something special; just don't tell the kids what it is until they eat it.

*Note: Some people cover the raw alligator with water and milk and soak it for a few hours before cooking it. They do not do that in jail but you can if you would like; it makes the meat tender. In jails, we have large steam kettles that tenderize everything and anything. (If you don't watch the inmates, they have been known to use the kettles to tenderize each other) You can also add a little red pepper or cayenne pepper for a little heat.

- 2 pounds alligator meat, trimmed and cubed
- 1 tablespoon vegetable oil
- 3 tablespoons minced garlic
- ½ cup onion, chopped
- ½ cup green peppers, chopped
- ½ cup celery, chopped
- 1 cup chicken broth
- 1 can (28 ounces) tomatoes & green chilies
- 2 teaspoons salt

- I teaspoon black pepper
- I teaspoon cumin
- I teaspoon oregano

1. Heat oil in a large, heavy pot. Sauté the alligator meat, garlic and onion until lightly brown.
2. Add the green peppers, celery, broth, tomatoes, salt, pepper, cumin and oregano.
3. Bring to a boil, then simmer, covered for 1-1 ½ hours until the meat is tender. Serve over cooked rice or mashed potatoes.

Sample menu for Florida: Submitted by Robert Cunningham, Food Service Coordinator, Retired

Breakfast: Orange juice, scrambled eggs, breakfast potatoes, bread and coffee

Lunch: Smoked sausage, au gratin potatoes, mixed vegetables, bread, butterscotch pudding

Dinner: Beef goulash, green beans, yellow cupcake, bread, margarine and milk.

Chapter 12

Middle of the Country and Further Out North

An historical fact; in those very old days, they cooked in a big kettle that always hung over the fire. Every morning they would add things to the pot. They ate mostly vegetables with not too much meat. They would eat stew for dinner, leaving the leftovers in the pot to get cold over night and then start over the next day. Sometimes the pot had food in it that had been there for quite a while. Hence the rhyme: 'Pease porridge hot, Pease porridge cold, Pease porridge in the pot, nine days old.' (I wonder how many people died from food poisoning)

MICHIGAN

FRESH FRUIT DESSERT PIZZA (Serves 6-8)

Canteen Food Services provides food and commissary services for 63 facilities in Michigan and Indiana. That is an average of 6,827 inmates per meal per day plus staff. This is a lot of people to keep happy, yes?

This recipe was submitted by Cindy Burns, Vice President of Correctional Services for Canteen Services. They make this for the staff and it is a big hit. This is one recipe I tested a few times just to make sure I had it right; it was SO good! It is great to serve after a spicy or heavy meal or anytime at all.

Preheat oven to 350 degrees

- 1 (14 ounce) can sweetened condensed milk
- 1 cup all purpose flour
- ½ cup sour cream
- 8 ounces cream cheese
- ¼ cup lemon juice
- 1 teaspoon vanilla
- ½ cup margarine, softened
- ¼ cup firmly packed brown sugar
- ¼ cup quick oats
- ¼ cup walnuts, finely chopped
- Fresh fruit; strawberries, kiwi, grapes

1. In a medium bowl, mix condensed milk, sour cream, cream cheese, lemon juice and vanilla. Mix well and chill.
2. In another bowl, beat margarine and sugar until fluffy. Mix in flour, oats and walnuts until well blended.
3. Press dough into a 12" circle on a lightly oiled pizza pan. Form a rim around the edge. Pierce dough well with a fork. Bake in a 375 degree oven for 10-12 minutes or until golden brown. Cool.
4. Spoon filling evenly onto the crust and arrange fruit slices on top. Chill before serving.

❧❧❧

Cindy shared this experience with me: "Canteen Services had offered me the first Correctional position in Michigan and I accepted. I left a secure job at a hospital to come to jail. At that time I was told that I had $.49 to spend on food and paper products per meal. It sounded low but I was up for the challenge. I was at the facility doing my initial paperwork and having my picture taken for my ID. The officer who took the picture must have weighed over 500 pounds and kept saying over and over; "We sure can't wait to get some good food in here; we have all been starving!" All of a sudden, my new career didn't look very promising and I was sure that the $.49 goal was unattainable. Nineteen years later, I am still here and so is that same officer!!"

Dawn Allan manages the foodservices for two Michigan county jails. She told me of two incidents that stood out in her mind that gives a good picture of life inside. "I came into work one day and witnessed a few officers assisting some inmates to medical. These guys were not capable of walking on their own. I asked the Sergeant what happened. He says he thinks they were *huffing* laundry soap. I said laundry soap? You have got to be kidding! The inmates were laundry workers and hall runners. They couldn't stand on their own.

They were throwing up and urinating on each other. The nurse comes in and checks them out and finds out they are drunk. The officers go check out the cell and find an empty fifth of whiskey bottle. Knowing that everyone is going to be accused in that cell, the inmates began to sing like canaries.

The inmates take out the trash and an officer goes out with them. One of the inmate's family put the bottle of whiskey on the back side of the dumpster. When the inmate took the trash out he overthrew a bag of trash and it went to the back of the dumpster. The inmate went around the back of the dumpster to get the bag and put the bottle in his pants. The sergeant did not pat them down as he was right out there with the inmates when they took the trash out. Now, of course, all inmates are patted down after taking out the trash." That is how we all "live and learn" in Corrections.

*Note: When the inmates do not have accommodating family members as in this case, they make their own liquor that is called Pruno in some places and Hooch in others. See Chapter 5 to see how they do it, in case you are so inclined. Also, since there are no pockets in inmates clothing, you wouldn't believe what they put down their pants. That inmate with the bottle in his pants had to be at the <u>very least</u> walking a little funny, don't you think?

Dawn also related this incident. "Another time, I had just gotten to work and was in the booking area getting my morning counts. A sergeant and an officer came in walking an inmate from his cell to the tank as he had been misbehaving. (A fact I didn't know at the time) I never turn my back on these guys so I was watching them as they came in. I shifted my weight to the other leg as he went to walk behind me. I no more did that when the officer I was talking to said "DON'T YOU DARE!" As soon as she said that, I instantly ducked down.

It is a good thing I did because the inmate had picked up the chair behind me and threw it over my head and it smashed into a printer. He was tackled to the floor by several officers. He was still fighting so they strapped him in the chair. (It is called the "race car") He was spitting at the officers so they put a spit cap on him. He was then put in a cell to face the wall. Wow; just a reminder to not turn your back or get comfortable." (I guess they have time out in jail too)

Note: Most jails have a discipline chair that is used for uncontrollable inmates as well as a face guard so they can't bite or spit on the staff. So much of the discipline seemed so juvenile to me at first but after a while I saw how it helped in controlling the situation in jail so that it is safer for everyone.

JAIL HOUSE BURRITO (Inmate style)

Dawn sent in this recipe that the inmates in Michigan make in their cells out of food they purchase through the commissary. I didn't try this one at home as even I would not want to taste it but you can if you like. (I put this in so you can see what some inmates do.)

- 1 snack size bag Doritos
- 1 snack size bag Cheetos
- 1 meat stick

- I package chili flavored rice
- I packet taco sauce

1. Mix rice according to the package and set aside. (this is like a single serving of instant flavored rice)
2. Smash the Doritos and Cheetos and mix them together. Put the mixture in one of the bags.
3. Break up the meat stick and put it in the bag; add the rice.
4. Fold the bag over; mix well and then top with taco sauce.

Note: It doesn't say but I am guessing that they roll it out on something to eat it or maybe just squeeze it out of the bag as they eat it. Yum!

Carla Fleming, Food Service Manager for Canteen Services, submitted these tidbits.

*One kitchen worker sent his teeth through our dishwasher. When we asked him why he did what he did, he said it was to clean them. (Of course, what a silly question)

*Our Assistant Manager went to wash her thermometer in a bucket of soapy water and hit something hard. Someone had put their tennis shoes in there as well. (You guessed it; to clean them.)

Cleanliness must be big in Michigan!

WISCONSIN

PIZZA CASSAROLE (Serves 8)

This recipe was submitted by Teddie Mitchell, Food Service Manager, Shawano, Wisconsin

*Note: This is the exact recipe from a Wisconsin jail. Variation: I would add ½ cup of grated parmesan cheese and 2 cups shredded mozzarella cheese on top before baking. I also would add 1 teaspoon black pepper and 1 teaspoon sugar to the spices. But that is just me since I am not in jail. Their inmates still like it without the cheese but I wouldn't; I am Italian. You also can add ½ cup sliced pepperoni to give it an extra zing. This is a great dish to put on a buffet or bring to a Scout camp picnic as kids love it!

Preheat oven to 350 degrees

- 1 pound ground beef
- ½ medium onion, chopped
- ½ green pepper, diced
- 1 can (8 ounces) mushroom stems and pieces, drained
- 1 can (14.5 ounces) tomato sauce
- 1 can (6 ounces) tomato paste
- 1 can (14.5 ounce) diced tomatoes
- 2 teaspoons pizza seasoning*
- 2 cups egg noodles or pasta, cooked

*Tip: If you can't find pizza seasoning, substitute the following:
½ teaspoon garlic powder, ½ teaspoon onion powder and ½ teaspoon dried oregano

1. In a Dutch oven or heavy pan, sauté the ground beef with the onions and peppers until no longer pink.
2. Stir in the mushrooms, tomato sauce, tomato paste, diced tomatoes and seasonings.
3. Mix in the egg noodles or pasta.
4. Pour mixture into a greased 12"x8" baking pan. Cover and bake for 20 minutes in a 350 degree oven.
5. Uncover and bake for 10-15 minutes longer.

A WORD ABOUT BEEF STEW

In almost, if not all, jails you will find some kind of beef stew and they are mostly the same recipe. I did find a few differences.

San Diego: We had the traditional stew; stew beef, white potatoes, carrots, celery, onions, garlic , seasonings and tomatoes, all cooked for a while until the beef gets tender. I found a similar recipe in a lot of states.

Florida: They use "beef crumbles", which is like the ground beef you see on pizza, along with tomato paste and frozen mixed vegetables.

Canada: Their recipe had diced beef chuck, turnips, onions, carrots, parsnips, zucchini, tomatoes, diced peppers, coriander, thyme, soy sauce and Worcestershire sauce. (Right up my alley)

Two mid West States: These folks didn't want me to even use their states, never mind their names. They serve "Road Kill Stew". I will try to do this as delicately as possible. The meat obviously varies with the time of year and the type of animals they receive. They were quick to add that the road kill was always fresh and of course free. It ranged from quail to bear to rabbit to possum to deer; they all added onions, garlic, potatoes and vegetables to their stews.

The jails sent out inmate work crews each day to see what they could find, especially during mating season. It seems that the animals run around a lot during this time and then get hit by cars. Talk about being frugal! The cooks told me that the inmates love the stews and the variety as well so they said, "Don't knock it till you try it". So I won't. My faithful tasters were happy I passed this up. It was only because I didn't know how to get some good road kill here in California. (Only kidding)

An historical fact; in the old days, those with money had plates made of pewter. Food with high acid content caused some of the lead to leach onto the food, causing death from lead poisoning. This happened most often with tomatoes, so for the next 400 years or so, tomatoes were considered poisonous. Lead cups were also used to drink ale or whiskey. The combination would knock some of them out for a few days. Sometimes they would be taken for dead and laid out on the kitchen table. The family would gather around and eat and drink and wait to see if they would wake up; hence the custom of holding a "wake".

NEW JERSEY

FRIED CHICKEN STRIPS OR CHICKEN FINGERS (Serves 4-6) Submitted by Richard Wyckoff, CCFP, Food Service Manager, retired

The original recipe called for Creole powder but I couldn't find that exact spice. So….I am sharing my Creole seasoning with you and I used it in place of the Creole powder. You can use this seasoning mix as a rub for anything from chicken to fish to beef. It gives it a little spice without the burn. However, if you like it hot, feel free to add more hot stuff to it such as more cayenne or red pepper flakes. When you are cooking for a large "captured" audience it is best to keep the spice to medium.

- *Creole Seasoning:
- 4 tablespoons cayenne pepper
- 2 tablespoons black pepper
- 2 tablespoons garlic powder

- 1 tablespoon onion powder
- 1 tablespoon salt
- 1 tablespoon paprika
- 1 tablespoon dried basil

1. Mix all together and store in a covered container.
2. You can substitute any kind of fish for the chicken. This is about the only and the best way to get inmates to eat fish. They normally do not like it broiled or baked but will generally eat anything fried.
3. In San Diego, we buy pre-browned, breaded fish filets then heat them and serve them with either tater tots (another favorite) and a mixed broccoli medley or with a flour tortilla, shredded cheese and refried beans for a fish taco. Cole slaw is a usual side dish.
4. In Canada, they use trout or perch for the fish and serve it with tartar sauce, mashed potatoes and green peas.
5. These chicken (or fish) strips are wonderful and addictive; great for kids and adults alike.

- ½ cup bread crumbs
- ½ cup cornflakes
- *1 tablespoon Creole seasoning
- ½ cup buttermilk
- 1 large egg
- 1 # raw skinless, boneless chicken breast
- ½ cup flour
- Vegetable oil for frying

1. Mix bread crumbs and cornflakes in a blender. Mix in the Creole seasoning. Place in a flat bowl.
2. Mix the buttermilk and egg in a separate bowl. (Hint: you can

make your own buttermilk by adding a tablespoon of white vinegar to regular or low-fat milk and let it sit 5 minutes.)

3. Cut the chicken breast into 1 inch strips.
4. Dip chicken strips in the flour, then the egg mixture and then the bread crumbs.
5. Fry in hot oil until golden brown, no more than seven pieces at a time. Drain on paper towels.
6. Serve with dipping sauces such as Barbeque Sauce or Sweet and Sour Sauce.

Sample menu for a New Jersey jail:

Breakfast: Orange juice, grits, turkey sausage, hash browns, bread, margarine, jelly, coffee, milk

Lunch: Sausage, spaghetti with tomato sauce, grated cheese, chopped broccoli, 2 slices bread, fresh orange, lemonade

Dinner: Fried Chicken tenders, peas and carrots, Spanish rice, 4 slices bread with margarine, peach crisp, iced tea

Chapter 13

Way Out West

Historical fact; in the old days, sometimes people could obtain pork which made them feel quite special. When visitors came over, they would hang up their bacon to show off. It was a sign of wealth that a man could, "bring home the bacon." They would cut off a little to share with guests and they would all sit around and chew the fat.

LA COUNTY SHERIFF, LOS ANGELES, CALIFORNIA

The LA County Sheriff's Food Services Unit operates 7 kitchens feeding *23,000* inmates, *87,000* meals per day. To give you an example of the massive amounts of food annually consumed by the inmates, they use 14 million cartons of milk (enough to fill an Olympic size swimming pool), 6.5 million cartons of orange juice, 46 million slices of bread and 913,000 pounds of lunch meat!

POZOLE SOUP (Serves 8-10);
Submitted by Maria Gonzales, Chief Cook,
Los Angeles County Sheriff

In jail, Pozole Soup is served "as is" with corn tortillas or crackers; however, you can serve garnishes on the side such as thinly sliced radishes, chopped cilantro and lime wedges. I like mine with shredded cheddar cheese but remember, I am Italian and love everything with cheese. I have Mexican friends who simmer this soup all day and all through the party people go get more and more. They also use some pork ribs as well as the meat and serve hot, spicy carrots on the side.

This is a filling, delicious soup and I hope that you enjoy it as much as they do in jail. I know the inmates in Virginia do not get this soup but then again we don't have that wonderful Peanut Soup in California jails; life is rough sometimes.

- 2 tablespoons vegetable oil
- 2 ½ pounds pork shoulder, cut into 1" pieces
- 1 large onion, chopped
- 4 cloves garlic, minced
- 1 can (15 ounce) cut tomatoes, not drained
- 1 can, (15 ounce) enchilada sauce
- 8 cups chicken broth
- 2 teaspoons oregano
- 2 teaspoons seasoned salt
- 1 tablespoon chili powder
- 3 cups canned hominy, drained

1. Heat the oil in a Dutch oven or large pot. Brown the pork pieces until light brown and remove and set aside.
2. Add the onion and garlic to the pot and lightly brown, about 3-4 minutes.
3. Return the pork to the pot; add the tomatoes, enchilada sauce, chicken broth, oregano, seasoned salt and chili powder.
4. Reduce heat to low and cook covered for 2 hours, stirring occasionally.
5. Add the hominy and cook for 15-20 minutes more. Taste the soup and correct the seasonings if necessary. Serve with lots of crusty bread for dipping.

Sample Menu for LA Jails:

Breakfast: Corn Flakes, 2 slices whole wheat bread, jelly, apple and milk.

Lunch: Smoked chicken lunch meat, 2 slices bread, mustard and mayo, apple, chocolate chip cookie, oriental mix and orange juice.

Dinner: Chicken-Vegetable burrito, chili beans, carrots, coleslaw, apple bar and milk.

SANTA ANA JAIL, CALIFORNIA

TURKEY NOODLE CASSAROLE WITH BROCCOLI (Serves 4) Submitted by Jeff Cullum, Food Service Manager, ARAMARK

You will find this recipe in many jails across the country in similar forms. In California State prisons, they use fettuccine noodles and add black pepper and parmesan cheese. In Minnesota jails, they add buttered bread crumbs and sometimes cheddar cheese on the top before baking in the oven. For a vegetarian dish, they leave out the turkey and add soy "chicken" pieces.

This is a tasty and satisfying dish that I know your family will love.

Preheat oven to 350 degrees.

- 8 ounces Rigatoni pasta
- 2 cups frozen Broccoli cuts
- 2 cups cooked turkey or chicken, bite size pieces
- I cup green or red peppers, chopped
- 4 ounces (I stick) margarine
- ½ cup all purpose flour

- 1 teaspoon salt
- 2 cups chicken broth

1. Cook the pasta in salted water, drain and set aside.
2. Mix the broccoli, turkey pieces and peppers into the noodles.
3. Melt the margarine in a medium pan; add the flour and stir until smooth. Cook, while stirring, for 2 minutes.
4. Slowly add the broth and salt and simmer for 15 minutes, stirring occasionally.
5. Combine the noodle mixture with the sauce; place in a buttered baking pan and bake in a 350 degree oven for 30 minutes.

CALIFORNIA STATE PRISONS
(Recipes submitted by Sue Summerset, Food Service Administrator, Retired)

Note: This book is about *Jail House* food but I thought a recipe from a prison would be interesting as well. The difference between jails and prisons is that when you are first arrested and go through the judicial procedures and/or trial, you stay in Detention facilities (jails). When you are sentenced, if you still have more than a year to serve you go "up the river" (as they say) to prison.

Many prisons have Prison Industries where they employ inmates doing a variety of jobs. California has a great program that employs approximately 5,900 inmates and operates over 60 manufacturing, service and agricultural industries in 22 prisons. They make anything from eyeglasses to shoes and of course license plates.

Many of the inmates have never held a job or learned the value of work. The inmates learn work skills and good habits that enhance their ability to obtain jobs upon their release from prison. In addition, it helps put our tax dollars to good use. As they say, "busy hands are happy hands".

Prison Industries farms over 500 acres of almond trees at two women's prisons. 75 inmates farm, package and distribute whole, sliced and diced almonds to the other state facilities. One of their favorite ways to use the almonds is in desserts as well as in a snack mix.

Approximately 100 inmates bone, grind and process in excess of *170,000* pounds of commercial beef a *week* at the meat and sausage plant in Mule Creek State Prison in Ione, California. They make bulk hamburger, patties, stew beef, bologna, franks and breakfast sausages. This is quite an operation! Some of their ground beef is used in the following recipe.

CHILI CONQUESTADOR (Serves 6)

The original recipe comes from the military recipe cards and it is a favorite of our people in uniform as well as the inmates. This is a very easy and filling main dish which is zesty and delicious. It is a bit warm so if you like it milder, leave out the red pepper.

They like to serve it in prison with a pineapple slaw which offsets the spices nicely. A fruit salad or ice cream will finish it off. Leftovers have known to be eaten right out of the refrigerator, even for breakfast.

Preheat oven to 375 degrees

- 1 ½ pounds ground beef
- 1 medium onion, diced
- 2 cans (14.5 ounces) diced tomatoes
- 1 tablespoon chili powder
- 1 tablespoon salt
- 1 tablespoon garlic powder
- 1 teaspoon red pepper

- ▪ 1 ½ cups cooked white rice
- ▪ 1 box Jiffy corn muffin mix

1. Brown the beef and onions in a heavy pan until no longer pink; drain off the fat.
2. Add the tomatoes, chili powder, salt, garlic powder and red pepper.
3. Cook over medium high heat for 5 minutes and then simmer for 15 minutes.
4. Add the rice and mix well.
5. Pour into an 8x12 baking pan.
6. Prepare the cornmeal batter as per the directions on the box.
7. Spoon the batter on top of the chili evenly over the mixture.
8. Bake in a 375 degree oven for 25 minutes or until the cornbread is done and brown.
9. Cut into wedges and serve hot.

*Note: You can make your own corn muffin mix as they do in prison instead of the Jiffy boxed mix but as you can tell, I am lazy.

Sample menu from the California Prisons:

Breakfast: Fresh fruit, oatmeal, waffles, 2 eggs, syrup, margarine, milk and coffee.

Lunch: Tuna salad sandwich, sunflower seeds, graham crackers, fresh fruit, punch

Dinner: Chili Conquistador, green beans, carrot and pineapple salad, cornbread, margarine, iced cake.

SACRAMENTO
(Submitted by Carol Heuer, Food Service Program Manager, Sacramento County Sheriff, California)

BROCCOLI CHEESE BAKE (Serves 6-8)

This recipe is used for those inmates on a Vegetarian diet in Sacramento jails. They are lucky people as this is a delicious dish that can be used as an entrée or a side dish. They are out of luck when they go to most other jails as they do not do *preference diets* unless a judge orders it. You can add other vegetables to this as well and the kids will be eating their veggies and loving it.

Preheat oven to 350 degrees

- 2 pounds fresh broccoli, trimmed and cut
- 2 tablespoons unsalted butter
- ¼ pound fresh mushrooms, sliced
- ¼ cup celery, chopped
- ¼ cup onion, chopped
- I can (8 ounces) water chestnuts, sliced
- I can (10 ¾ ounce) cream of mushroom soup
- 8 ounces cream cheese
- ½ teaspoon garlic salt
- ½ teaspoon black pepper
- I cup grated cheddar cheese

1. Steam broccoli until tender.
2. Melt butter in a medium skillet and sauté the mushrooms, celery and onion until softened.
3. Combine the broccoli with the water chestnuts, stir in the onion mixture and set aside.

4. Heat the soup and the cream cheese in a pot over low heat until the cheese melts. Add the garlic salt and pepper. Pour it over the broccoli mix and combine.

5. Put into a 9x13 pan that has been sprayed with a non stick spray and bake for 20-25 minutes in a 350 degree oven.

6. Sprinkle the top with the grated cheese during the last 5 minutes of baking.

Sample menu for Sacramento Jail:
Breakfast: Fresh fruit, wheat cereal, scrambled eggs, hash browns, 2 slices ww bread, milk and hot tea.
Lunch: Minestrone soup, croutons, peanut butter and jelly sandwich, fresh fruit, and iced tea.
Dinner: Baked meatloaf, brown gravy, macaroni and cheese, carrots, tossed salad with dressing, 2 slices bread, layer cake and iced tea.

ORANGE COUNTY, CALIFORNIA

BEANS CHARROS (Cowboy Beans),
Submitted by Senior Cook Marcelo Jimenez,
Orange County Sheriff

In many of our jails we use some soy products in our recipes. Some jails make dishes with soy in them for their vegetarian diets. Some people use soy in place of ground beef if they can get it cheaper or if they want to reduce the fat content of their menu. In San Diego we only occasionally used soy as it wasn't cheaper than beef or ground turkey. Also, we did not offer vegetarian diets to our inmates.

Using soy products is very healthy and they have come a long way in improving the taste and the look of their products. I remember the hamburger patties of my youth in school that had TVP added to it; little gray flecks of soy bean was all through the patty. No way would inmates eat anything with gray in it nor did I. Now you wouldn't even know soy was in the patty.

These beans are really good and are a great accompaniment to all kinds of meats and Mexican food. Here's a little history for you. Charros were the elegant horsemen of Mexico, but later the term was used to describe the Mexican cowboys who settled and worked in Texas. These beans would be simmering in an earthenware olla on the back of the stove or over the open fire on the range.

The regular recipe calls for cooked, chopped chorizo and chopped bacon instead of soy sausage.

Serve with shredded cheddar cheese, tortillas, tomato salsa and Jalapenos. It is a meal by itself.

- I can, 16 ounces, cooked pinto beans (you can start with dry pinto beans and cook them if you wish)
- ½ medium onion, chopped
- ½ green pepper, diced
- 5 cloves garlic, chopped
- I can, 14.5 ounces, diced tomatoes
- ½ teaspoon salt
- ½ teaspoon Mexican oregano
- ½ teaspoon ground cumin
- ½ teaspoon paprika
- ½ teaspoon chili powder
- 8 ounces soy sausage*

1. Place cooked pinto beans in a medium pot over medium heat.
2. Add all other ingredients except soy sausage and mix well.
3. Simmer over very low heat for 30 minutes, stirring occasionally.
4. In a skillet, cook the soy sausage, breaking it into crumbles.

5. Add the soy sausage crumbles to the beans and cook another 15 minutes. For more heat you can add a small amount of Tabasco sauce.

6. If the beans become dry, add a small amount of water until you reach the right consistency.

*Note: I used "Gimmie Lean Sausage" by Lightlife. It only comes in a 14 ounce package so I reserved 6 ounces and used it in a tomato sauce. You can double this recipe and use the whole package if you wish.

ARIZONA

MENUDO (Serves 8)

*Note: This is a jail recipe. You can add 1 teaspoon coriander, roasted chili peppers or hot sauce to add more heat. In step 1, some people add veal or beef knuckles to the tripe and remove the bones at the end of the cooking cycle before adding the hominy to give it extra flavor.

Menudo is very popular in Mexico for a variety of reasons, the main one being that it is a very hearty and comforting stew. It is commonly used for hangovers and is known to sooth the senses as well as the stomach. My Mexican friends tell me this is true but tripe is not the first thing *I* think of when my stomach needs soothing. It is more like Italian bread and chicken soup; to each their own, yes?

It is very popular in the Arizona jails that serve it. Even though the inmates have very few hangovers to worry about, it is still comforting. This dish takes a while to cook at home but it is a lot faster in the jails where they have large steam kettles. Serve this stew with flour tortillas and a salad.

- 2 pounds beef tripe, cut in 1 inch pieces
- 6 cups water
- 2 medium onions, chopped
- 1 tablespoon garlic powder
- 2 teaspoons salt
- 1 tablespoon black pepper
- 1 tablespoon dried oregano
- 1 tablespoon red pepper flakes
- 2 (15 ounce) cans hominy, not drained

1. Place tripe pieces, water, onions, garlic powder, salt, black pepper, oregano and red pepper flakes in a Dutch oven.
2. Bring to a boil, cover and simmer for 3 hours until the tripe has a clear, jelly like appearance. Periodically skim off the fat.
3. Add the hominy and simmer 15 minutes.

INDIAN FRY BREAD

Indian Fry Bread is a lot like tortillas but different in texture. This recipe is Navajo and used in the jails I spoke to but there are also recipes from other tribes that have slight variations. Fry Bread has an interesting history behind it.

The Navajo developed it during the four years of captivity in the 1860's when they were put into camps after the 300 mile walk from their home land. They made use of the government supplies of lard, flour, salt, baking powder, and powdered milk. To some, Indian Fry Bread is a sacred tradition; it is to be consumed by the "People" until the earth is again purified. It is a favorite to be consumed in jail and the way things look, it will be for a long time.

- 1 cup unbleached flour

- ¼ cup powdered nonfat milk
- I teaspoon baking powder
- ¼ teaspoon salt
- ½ cup warm water
- Vegetable oil for frying

1. Sift together the flour, powdered milk, baking powder and salt in a large bowl.
2. Pour the water over the flour mixture and stir the mixture with a fork until it forms a ball.
3. With floured hands on a floured board, mix the dough until it forms a floured ball. Do not knead the dough as it will become tough. Let stand 1 hour.
4. Shape the dough into small balls and pat out into circles.
5. Heat the oil in a cast iron or large skillet to about 350 degrees.
6. Fry the circles of dough on both sides until light brown, pressing down on the circle so the oil covers the dough while it is frying. Drain on paper towels.
7. They can be served with honey, cinnamon sugar or jam for breakfast or dessert. To make an Indian taco, put taco meat, shredded lettuce and shredded cheddar cheese on the top of the fry bread and serve with chopped onions and sour cream on the side.

I can't talk about Arizona without talking about Sheriff Joe Arpaio with the Maricopa County Sheriff's Department. He is well known for his tent cities where he houses the overflow from the jails in over 100 degree temperatures. When the inmates complain he tells them that our soldiers in Iraq live in tents in 120 degrees, wear full body armor and haven't committed a crime so "shut up". He is tough on inmates and his methods are applauded by most other law enforcement.

For instance, he has a volunteer female chain gang. Chained

together by the ankle, they pick up trash on the roads and bury bodies in the County cemetery, all to get out of sitting in a cell. I can't think of anything else I would rather do then bury bodies!

The inmates wear the old fashioned black and white striped uniforms and of course the famous pink underwear and socks. It caught on so well that big stores in the area are selling pink underwear for men by the thousands.

When told by the courts that he had to provide TV to the inmates, he complied but he chose the channels which are mostly Disney and educational programs. And that is if they behave! Most jails use TV privileges as a behavior modification tool and it works.

Sheriff Joe has his own radio station, KJOE, which broadcasts in the jails, 5 days a week, four hours a day. It plays classical music, opera, Frank Sinatra, patriotic music and educational programming. (Sounds good to me)

As far as Food Services go, Sheriff Joe feeds the inmates 2500 calories per day in only *2 meals a day*. In the morning they receive a clear plastic bag that contains cold cereal, bread, bologna or some other lunch meat, a peanut butter pack, fresh fruit, chips or a cookie and milk.

At night they receive a hot dinner meal that consists of some kind of casserole dish, such as stew, vegetables, a roll, some kind of salad and fruit. Sheriff Joe is fond of saying that he serves green bologna and doesn't much care for niceties, such as coffee, salt, pepper or catsup, when it comes to their food. His cost per meal is one of the cheapest in the nation.

However, he did spend millions of dollars to build an 187,000 square foot, state of the art Production Center where they use the Cook/Chill method to insure the safety and sanitation of the food process. They have some huge processing machines; for instance there is one that looks like a large cement mixer and all it does is remove the strings from *tons* of green beans. It creates quite a mess but gets the job done. Over 10,000 inmates eat a heck of a lot of green beans.

They also send out trucks to get produce donations from farmers and have volunteer chain gangs that glean the fields. They did build a cannery and a dehydration plant to use these donations but it remains dormant at this time. So when they get a particular vegetable in season, the inmates get to eat that vegetable every day until it is gone. So much for variety; most of the things Sheriff Joe does would not be possible in California due to our regulations.

I am not including a recipe from there because I really didn't see anything that was that good or unique when it comes to jail house food at Sheriff Joe's place.

The morale of the story is "go to jail in California!" Nine out of ten inmates like our food in California the best. It is so nice to be loved.

Chapter 14

Get Out of Town

Tis the Desert that graces all the Feast,
for an ill end disparages the rest....
an 18th century poet.

I thought you would like to see what some other countries have for food in case you ever run into a problem while traveling. If you go to Australia you will be OK since their rules that govern food in jails is very similar to our rules. However, I think you may want to think twice about misbehaving in some of the Arab countries.

I had some gentlemen from an Arab country visit me at old Central jail to talk to me about the use of cook/chill for restaurants in their country. We got on the elevator with the normal load of chained inmates in the back and my guests seemed very uncomfortable. The deputy told the inmates to face the back and my guests turned as well. I told them he did not mean it for them. I could tell that they were not used to being around inmates as they were very edgy and nervous.

When we were in my office, I asked them if they had many jails in their country and they said "no". When I asked why not they told me that their system of justice was much better than ours so they had little need to detain people for long. I had heard about the removal of hands, feet and other parts of the body for crimes as well as an almost instant death sentence.

After a while they told me that the other reason crime is kept down is that they control two things; the use of liquor and their women. Yet they had come to *this woman* for advice. I did not take offence at what they said and gave them the information they needed anyway. It takes all kinds, yes?

BELGIUM

GENTSE WATERZOOI (Serves 8-10)

I have given you this recipe as it is prepared for use in a restaurant or at home. In the jails, they mix bite size pieces of chicken into the sauce and vegetables and of course there is no layering of ingredients or garnish. The potatoes are served on the side. Also, they usually use milk instead of cream.

There is a lot of interesting history that goes with this recipe. It was originally a dish made to serve to the poor and is a classic stew of Flanders. Its' name is Dutch from "zooien", meaning to boil. In archaic Dutch it means "watery mess" which it is not! I found it to be very tasty with the fresh taste of the vegetables, tender chicken and smooth sauce.

It is known as comfort food and I certainly felt comforted. Julia Child and Rachael Ray both discovered this dish and made their versions of it which included the addition of *vermouth*. I think the inmates would have liked their recipes, especially the vermouth part.

I also discovered that French fries originated in Belgium, believe it or not. Their National dish is steak, fries and salad or fries and mussels which I am sure the inmates would appreciate as well if they could get it. I guess that is for the rich people; I would still be happy with Waterzooi instead. . I serve it with crusty French bread and since it is so rich and filling, it was a meal onto itself.

- 2 green zucchini
- I pound fresh carrots
- 4 stalks celery
- I large leek
- ½ large onion
- 5 cups vegetable stock or chicken stock
- 2 pounds fresh potatoes, any kind

- 2-3 pounds boneless, skinless chicken, breasts or thighs or mixed, cut into a medium pieces
- 4 tablespoons margarine
- 4 tablespoons flour
- I pint half and half
- 2 egg yolks, beaten
- I teaspoon white pepper
- I teaspoon salt
- Fresh parsley for garnish

1. Thinly slice the zucchini, carrots, celery and leek. Chop the onion.
2. Place the vegetable stock in a large heavy pot; add the vegetables. Bring to a boil and simmer for 10 minutes.
3. Remove the vegetables and keep warm.
4. Poach the chicken pieces in the broth for about 15 minutes or until just cooked.
5. Remove the chicken, set aside and keep warm.
6. Boil the potatoes in a separate pot. Drain and cut into bite sized pieces and keep warm.
7. Make a roux with the margarine and flour; melt the margarine in a small pan, whisk in the flour and cook for 2 minutes. Add 2 cups of the vegetable broth and cook until thickened.
8. Add the roux mixture to the remaining broth and cook 5 minutes.
9. Add the cream, the egg yolks and salt and pepper; cook for 5 minutes. Add the vegetables and cook another 5 minutes.
10. For serving, place a small amount of potatoes in each bowl. Ladle the vegetables and sauce on the top of the potatoes and then place pieces of chicken on top of the vegetables. Garnish with chopped parsley.

PROVINCE OF ONTARIO, CANADA

In 1995, I did a consulting job for the Ministry of Justice for the Province of Ontario. I helped them develop a Central Kitchen to use Cook/Chill technology to prepare their food for their jails and prisons. I visited many of their institutions and I was very impressed with their staff. From their Chief, Nancy Guppy, to their great supervisors and cooks, they could not have been nicer to me.

I was very impressed to hear how dedicated they were to their facilities. It seems that every so often the unions go on strike and everything closes down. The staff is required to remain in the facilities for as long as weeks at a time with limited food choices as almost nothing goes in or out of the facilities during a strike. After hearing what they have to go through, I didn't complain any more for being locked down for a day in my jails. At least I did not have to sleep there.

TEA CAKES (Yield: 15-16 cakes)

On some days in the jails in Toronto, Canada, tea cakes are on the menu for breakfast. They also serve inmates tea with each meal. The morning after I baked these cakes, I sat and had some with my tea and thought that this would be very pleasant, even if I *were* in jail. These little cakes are similar to scones and just sweet enough. Be careful, they could become addictive.

Preheat oven to 375 degrees

- 1 ½ cups all purpose flour
- ½ cup sugar
- ½ teaspoon salt
- 2 teaspoons baking powder
- ½ cup butter or margarine, semi-soft
- ½ cup dried currents
- 1 large egg
- 1 teaspoon vanilla extract
- 2 tablespoons milk, regular or low fat
- Granulated sugar

1. Sift together the flour, sugar, salt and baking powder into a large bowl.
2. Work the butter into the flour mixture with your fingers.
3. Mix in the currents.
4. In a small bowl, beat the egg; reserve a tablespoon of egg for glazing the cakes.
5. Add the vanilla and milk to the egg and mix.
6. Add the egg mixture to the flour and mix with a spoon to form dough.
7. Drop the dough by tablespoon and form a ball. Place the balls on a buttered sheet pan and flatten them a little.
8. Glaze the top of each one with the reserved egg and sprinkle each one with sugar.
9. Bake at 375 degrees for approximately 13-15 minutes or until lightly brown on top and brown around the edges. (They do not spread) Place them on a rack to cool and then store them in a covered container. These can be eaten warm or cold; they are still delicious!

LENTIL AND RICE SOUP (Serves 6-8)
Submitted by David Sharma, Food Service Manager, Hamilton, Ontario Corrections

This is a delicious, filling soup. They serve it with Perogies, fried onions, cheese sauce, carrots and pudding which is a bit different than here in the US. We usually serve it with crackers, a sandwich, a salad of some kind and a cookie. It sounds more exotic in Canada, aye? So I have included the Perogi recipe as well. I want you to have an authentic Canadian *jail house food night.*

- 8 cups chicken broth
- 2 cups lentils
- I can (14.5 ounces) diced tomatoes
- 2 large white potatoes, cubed
- I medium onion, chopped
- 2 stalks celery, chopped
- 2 large carrots, diced
- 2 teaspoons black pepper
- I bay leaf
- I tablespoon granulated sugar

1. Simmer lentils in chicken broth, in a covered soup pot, for 45 minutes or until tender.
2. Add the rest of the ingredients; bring to a boil.
3. Reduce heat and simmer, covered for 30 minutes or until vegetables are tender.

PEROGIES (POLISH DUMPLINGS) (Yields 40)

In jail they top these delectable dumplings with fried onions and a cheese sauce. There are other fillings you could use such as drained sauerkraut, browned with some chopped mushrooms, salt and pepper and a little sugar. These little things are so good that 40 of them never seem enough for everyone. Enjoy them as appetizers or a complete meal with vegetables, salad or soup.

Dough:
- 1 cup all purpose flour
- 1 large egg
- ¼ teaspoon salt
- 4 tablespoons cold water, approximately
- Melted butter

1. Mix all ingredients, except the butter, together to form medium—soft dough.
2. Knead well and roll out on a floured board until thin. Cut into about 40 circles using a glass or cookie cutter.
3. Moisten the edges of the circles with a little water and spoon some filling into the center. Fold the circles over into ½ circles and press to seal the edges.
4. To cook, drop them into salted, boiling water, one at a time and cook, covered, until they all float to the top, about 10 minutes. Cook, still covered, for 5 minutes longer.
5. Drain and place on a heated platter; drizzle a little melted butter over the top of them.

Filling:
- 1 large potato, cooked and mashed
- ¼ medium onion, chopped and browned

- I tablespoon melted butter
- 2 tablespoons cottage cheese, drained
- Salt and pepper to taste

1. Mix all the ingredients together and then use the mixture to stuff the dough.

Sample menu for Ontario Province:
Breakfast: Apple juice, cold cereal, 2 tea biscuits, peanut butter and jelly, whole wheat toast, tea and milk
Lunch: Lentil soup, perogies, fried onions, cheese sauce, carrots, whole wheat bread, pudding and tea
Dinner: Breaded trout nuggets, mashed potatoes, green peas, whole wheat bread, applesauce and tea

ENGLAND

BANGERS AND MASH

In Great Britain, they have 18 correctional institutions administered by the government that serve approximately 19,000 inmates a day. They have other institutions that are operated by private companies as well. The government uses Cook/Chill technology to prepare some of their food and they distribute it to their facilities.

The UK's rules and regulations, as well as the mandated caloric and nutritional values, are almost the same as ours here in the U.S. Their costs are similar at $2.00-$2.50 per inmate per day. The dishes are very similar as well; it is just that some of them are presented in a different way.

This is one of their favorite recipes and is well accepted by the inmates. They serve it with mushy peas, carrots, applesauce and bread. Here in the States, we serve the sausage separately with no onions, and the potatoes and gravy on the side and maybe with peas, not necessarily mushy. We also give them a hot dog bun or bread so they can make a sandwich. Many jails use hot dogs, not sausages. Our English friends should *sort of* feel right at home here.

Preheat oven to 350 degrees

- 2 pounds white potatoes, peeled and cubed
- 1 tablespoon chicken base
- 4 ounces (1 stick) butter
- 1 cup milk
- 1 teaspoon white pepper
- 8 pork, turkey or chicken sausages
- 1 large onion, cut in rings
- 1 can (10.5 ounce) beef gravy

1. Place the potatoes in a medium saucepan and cover with water. Boil until tender and drain.
2. Add the chicken base, butter, milk and white pepper. Mash the potatoes and keep warm.
3. Place the sausages in a baking pan, cover with the onion rings, and bake in a 350 degree oven for 20 minutes.
4. Heat the gravy in a small saucepan and set aside.
5. Spread the mashed potatoes on top of the sausages and continue baking for 15 minutes. Serve each person 2 sausages with some of the potatoes and the brown gravy on top.

PUERTO RICO

Many recipes from Puerto Rico call for these two ingredients; adobo seasoning and sofrito so I have included them here for you.

ADOBO SEASONING

- 3 tablespoons salt
- I tablespoon onion powder
- I tablespoon garlic powder
- I tablespoon black pepper
- ½ teaspoon oregano
- ½ teaspoon chili powder
- ½ teaspoon cumin

1. Mix all ingredients together and store in a container with a tight lid in a cool dry place.
2. This seasoning can also be used in Mexican dishes as well as a rub for meat, chicken or fish.

SOFRITO

- ½ medium green pepper, chopped
- ½ medium sweet red pepper, chopped
- I large tomato, chopped
- 2 medium onions, chopped
- ½ head garlic, peeled
- ½ bunch cilantro, chopped

1. Place all ingredients in a blender or food processor and blend. Makes one pint.

RICE AND GREEN PIGEON PEAS (Serves 8)

Sofrito is used in a dish called Rice and Green Pigeon Peas. Pigeon Peas are also known as gandules. I found them in cans in a Puerto Rican food store. I also made it with frozen green peas; it was good but not quite the same or as exotic sounding as "pigeon peas". This dish is very versatile and can be served with almost anything like roast meats, enchiladas, chicken or sausages.

- 1/3 cup sofrito
- 2 tablespoons vegetable oil
- 3 cups beef stock
- 2 cups raw rice
- 2 tablespoons tomato sauce
- ½ teaspoon salt
- I can, (12 ounces) gandules, not drained

1. In a deep pot simmer the sofrito in the oil for 2 minutes, stirring constantly.
2. Add the broth, rice, tomato sauce and salt; mix well.
3. Cook on high heat until the water evaporates and the surface of the rice is exposed but not completely dry. Add the gandules or peas.
4. Lower the heat to low and cook for 20 minutes.
5. Uncover the pot, making sure the condensate does not fall back into the pot as this could make the rice soggy. Using a large spoon, gently turn the rice over towards the center, turning the pot as you go. The rice should be tender. If not, return to the heat and cook for several more minutes. Turn and test the rice again to assure that it is done.

CHICKEN AND RICE (Serves 6)

This chicken dish is so good and very easy to make. I did not have any trouble getting my tasters to taste it. In fact, I now use the adobo seasoning and Sofrito in other recipes as well.

These recipes were submitted by Dennis Lopez, Canteen Food Services Regional Manager for Puerto Rico and the Virgin Islands. He said that chicken is one of the inmates' favorite meals as it is in the U.S. I always thought that their food was spicy hot but not so. They serve it with vegetables and fruit for dessert. This dish does very well at a pot luck supper.

- 1 whole chicken, cut into serving pieces
- Adobo seasoning
- 2 tablespoons vegetable oil
- 1 ½ cups Sofrito
- 3 ½ cups water
- 3 cups white uncooked rice

1. Rub the chicken pieces with adobo seasoning.
2. Heat the oil in a large pot. Sauté the chicken until light brown.
3. Add the Sofrito and cook for 10 minutes over medium heat.
4. Add the water and bring to a boil. Add the rice.
5. When it begins to boil again, lower the heat, cover and simmer for approximately 20 minutes, stirring occasionally.

Please see the sample daily menu below. They sure eat well down there in Puerto Rico behind bars.

Breakfast: Oatmeal or farina with milk, Criollo bread (Similar to

Italian bread), margarine and a slice of yellow cheese and coffee.

Lunch: Chicken and rice, carrot salad, sliced peaches and fruit drink.

Dinner: Baked Pork Chop "A la Jardinière" (or "Garden Style" Vegetables), steamed white rice, pink beans stewed with calabaza (local squash), Dinner roll, margarine, applesauce and a vanilla milkshake

Chapter 15

One Can Always Use Good "PR"

Historical fact; bread was divided according to status. Workers got the burnt bottom of the loaf, the family got the middle and guests got the top, or the "upper crust".

I have always believed in good public relations and maintaining a good public image. I also believed that we in San Diego defined the "upper crust" in correctional food services and we worked hard every day to keep it that way. Every six months or so, our food service was either on TV or in the newspaper or being written up in trade magazines. It really made all three of the Sheriffs I worked for over the years very happy to be shown in a good light.

It is normal that the good things that law enforcement does go unreported. The public needs to know that the services that are paid for by their taxes are working as efficiently and effectively as possible. I did my best to make sure it happened.

There are various ways to create good PR; one of the most effective was to be featured on TV. We were very fortunate to be featured several times over the years. In preparing to write this chapter, I reviewed the taped programs and in some ways it was kind of painful. For over 20 years at least 4 channels featured our food service. Here I was so young and then there I was older and then older still; it was like watching a time machine movie.

Two of my favorite ones were with Rod Luck from KUSI; they were 5 years apart and we grew older together. Right before the second program in 2000 was filmed, I kind of yelled at Rod. I had just walked onto the Production Floor and I saw this inmate in a tan uniform leaning on my kettle which was full of food and in operation.

First of all, inmates who were allowed in the kitchen wore *white* uniforms and this inmate was out of place. Then there was the fact that we allow *no one* to lean on our kettles; not only is it dangerous but very unsanitary. So....I did what I usually do. I called out to him and said, "Trustee, get off my kettle!"

Rod, who is a spirited guy, jumped back, put his hands up, assumed the position on the nearest wall and started to apologize. By this time, I was right up to him and I could see who it was. What a great way to start production, yes? Who knew he would be in an inmate's uniform but that's Rod; he really got into his work. He forgave me, thank goodness, and we went on to do a great program.

The programs started out talking a lot about the state of the art machines in our production center; all of them marveling at the control, sanitation and quality of the food and the vast amount of produced meals. (42,000 per day) It then became apparent to them we were in the minority in the correctional field as we cared so much about the quality and consistency of the meals for the inmates and staff.

The hosts started to emphasize this aspect of our food services and they were all very complimentary to us. They realized I was on a "one woman crusade" to improve jail food; one of them called me a combination of Betty Crocker, Colonel Sanders and Marie Calendar, all rolled into one.

They acknowledged the fact that we were internationally known and people from all over the world from all different disciplines were duplicating our procedures. The last program was done in 2006; Jack Gates exclaimed that we mixed "home style cooking" with mass production; he had it in a nutshell. It was selected as one of the most favorite programs of the year and as a consequence, they ran it for 6 more weeks into 2007. It was a real morale booster for our staff to be recognized by our home town.

As an International speaker and lecturer, I promoted what we were doing in San Diego to improve food service in corrections. I did many presentations to all kinds of organizations who had never even thought about the food in jails not to mention the use of the new technology available to our industry to make our food better and safer to eat. One of my favorite openings for my speeches was; "I have good news and bad news and they are both the same; Business is Booming in Corrections".

In addition, I have been a guest lecturer at San Diego State University for the past 20 years and I coordinated a lecture series to support the Culinary Program at St. Vincent De Paul in San Diego. For many years I was on the advisory committee for the San Diego Art Institute as the PAC Emeritus for their Culinary Program and I lectured there as well. I absolutely love working with all those wonderful students; they give us hope for the future.

There were several articles written about us in the San Diego Union and the San Diego Reader which were all very complimentary. In addition, over 100 articles in Food Service Trade Magazines over the years featured our operation. Needless to say we became very well known and all in a good way. Creating what? Good PR.

One of my favorite articles was written by Eleanor Widmer for the San Diego Reader in July, 1995. Eleanor was a restaurant critic and TV personality and a real trip! She was talking with Alvin and Laura Friedman, two of my dear friends, who told her about how wonderful our food was so she came to critique our operation and food. This was really unusual as food critics *never* critique jailhouse cuisine.

I toured her through our Production Center where she sampled all the food we were cooking and baking that day, all the while holding onto my arm for dear life. So I was very surprised when she said that she would like to sit with the 40 kitchen inmates while they had lunch. She wrote that it was the highlight of her day and how great the food was in detail, just like she was reviewing a restaurant.

Two of the inmates she spoke with during lunch told her they liked the food but it wasn't what they were used to eating. They told her that their family was in the high end restaurant business and they missed their seafood and steak. They also told her they were very impressed by our organization, attention to detail and sanitation and would be taking this knowledge back to their family business; high praise indeed. You would have thought I set it up but I didn't even know these guys were in jail, never mind my kitchen; they were in jail under aliases.

You would think that she would be full by now but no; she wanted to eat in a *real jail*. We went to the East Mesa Jail, which is behind the Production Center, for a second lunch, with Eleanor still firmly attached to my arm. Eleanor was a slim lady in her early seventies; I have never seen anyone *eat that much* in such a short period of time. She said she was used to doing this as she needed to sample many of the dishes at a restaurant in order to do a good review.

She wrote a wonderful article, praising everything she ate and saw that day; I truly believe she really enjoyed herself and we were happy that she did!

There was a reporter for the San Diego Tribune who also did a spot on a local radio show. He wrote a small item in his column about how an inmate had called him and told him how much he liked the Hagan Das ice cream he had in jail. Of course, everyone got the wrong idea and we were the talk of the town. I immediately called him and explained the company had shut down one of their warehouses and had practically given the ice cream away to us as a one-time deal. The ice cream was served in place of a dairy menu item which would have cost us much more so it actually saved money and raised the inmates' morale at the same time.

I convinced him to tell everyone on his radio spot the *last* part to the story. So he did. Sometimes you are damned if you do and damned if you don't; there is always that fine line when dealing with the public.

In another incident, the Navy called us and wanted to donate a bunch of food items they had in the freezer of a ship that was being de-commissioned. The only two conditions were we had to pick it up immediately and we had to take everything. Never one to turn down free food, we sent our truck down to the ship. The Navy was happy to be able to donate the food and we were happy to get it.

When I looked at the list of food that was donated I almost had a heart attack. Among other items like beans, flour and sugar were lobster tails, shrimp and steak! Since donated food must be served to the inmates we had a real problem on our hands. Some of the public wouldn't care if it was free or not; there would be quite a fuss. So....I informed my Commander of the situation and told him we had devised recipes to disguise the food as much as possible. I wanted him to know in case things back-fired but it all worked out OK.

It really hurt me to have the steak sliced and used as beef tips over noodles but it came out great and no one knew the difference. We made Seafood Newburg with the lobster and shrimp which really pained me the most. Most of the staff volunteered to stay late to boil the tails and shrimp and peel and chop them up. (I am sure there was a *little tasting* here and there.) We mixed in some of our regular fish and it turned out to be one of the best New Years Day dinners ever and no one was the wiser. You do what you got to do, yes? I just know that there are x-inmates out there reading this and saying, "No wonder it was so good!"

You know you have good food when the Sheriff auctions off "Lunch with the Sheriff at the Jail" at various charity fund raisers. We never cooked anything special for these occasions and did not know the Sheriff was coming to dine with the staff until he and his guests showed up. The winners were always very complimentary about the food, the staff, how clean our kitchens were and the politeness of the inmate workers. It created good PR for everyone.

Another way to promote good PR was to use our resources to assist the County in emergency situations. The Sheriff had a great Emergency Services Division which, among other things, conducted searches for lost people as well as provided assistance in all emergencies such as accidents, earthquakes, floods and fires. They operated a "roach coach", which is a kitchen on wheels. We trained their volunteer staff and kept them stocked with food.

As I was on 24 hour call, I received many 2:00 am calls from their Lieutenant to provide perishable food for their incidents. (I am here to tell you that most people get lost at night for some odd reason) We would work out the menu for 100-200 people and I would set up the food at the nearest jail for them to pick up. They were a great group of guys and gals who provided relief to hundreds of people and we were glad to help.

A great example was the support we provided during the 2001 Biotech Convention. Since there were riots and civil unrest in another city the year before, law enforcement was in full swing in San Diego to provide safety to everyone. There were many police officers and sheriff deputies from many other cities joining forces with our officers. We were charged with feeding our sheriffs during this three day period so we figured out a way to do it.

Assistant Chief Hans Ludwig and his crew set up a food camp at NTC, a mostly vacant Navy facility down by the airport. We had a generator brought in to run the refrigerators and warming ovens we had moved onto the site. In the meantime, Assistant Chief Paul Benitez and his staff cooked and packaged the extra meals needed to feed everyone.

The LAPD were staying in the old barracks on base so we fed them along with the SDPD guarding the gates and of course the sheriffs in the field. When Hans found out that the LAPD needed breakfast as well, he provided these meals for them. They gave him some cigars at the end to say thanks. All the PD people were very surprised that the food was so good and were very appreciative. Little did they know they were *eating jail house meals*. Our Sheriff, Bill Kolender was Very happy and that is what counts!

Of all the missions we had over the years, one incident will stand out in my mind forever; San Diego Fire Storm, 2003. The sky was heavy grey; a red sun was shining dully through the grey and white silt. The whole city was up in flames in different spots—a circle of three fires spreading down towards the sea with the devil winds blowing in at 40 mph.

When I walked out of my house at 6:00 that morning, I thought it was snowing. Then I realized ashes were falling like dirty snow; dirt and grit were two inches deep on the ground. It was pure hell; cars and homes were burned to the ground, all the trees going up like torches and wild animals and horses running for their lives.

I immediately went back in the house and called Assistant Chief Paul Benitez, who put our emergency plan into action. Paul went to the Central Production Center with one of our drivers, packed a truck with food and supplies and our brave driver raced around the spreading fires to where the first responders had set up a camp in Lakeside.

We provided thousands of meals through the next five days in various locations, providing much needed assistance to these brave men and women. In the meantime, we had to evacuate some of the jails and camps so food and staff needed to be re-directed to other facilities. My wonderful staff pulled together, working long tiring hours to make it happen.

While Paul handled the Central Production Center and the production of more food, Hans made the rounds of all the facilities and facilitated the movement of supplies. He even went to check one of our facilities in the mountains which had been evacuated to assure that all was secured.

Hans sent me pictures of the fire that was literally right up to the jail fences; I realized that these people were extremely brave. Our truck drivers continued to deliver food and supplies to everyone, including the firemen and law enforcement working the fires, despite the adverse conditions and the danger that was all around them. And not one of them complained!

One of our drivers, George Abi-Najm, volunteered to bring food into Julian, a town in the mountains which was literally surrounded by the fire. The firemen and sheriffs had encircled the town and were fighting to keep it safe but were almost out of cooked food. When I spoke to George, who is a native of Lebanon, about the dangers he faced, he said that as long as they weren't *shooting* at him, he could deal with a little fire. Since we were the ones with the guns it was OK to go.

He literally drove around areas of fire, talking his way through the check points, until he found a way into Julian. Boy, were they glad to see him and all the wonderful hot food he brought with him. I wasn't a bit surprised; George and my staff were always willing to go the extra mile. Julian was saved and I like to think we had a small part in it, especially George.

All my staff went those extra miles throughout the week, all without complaint. It was times like these which made me realize what a great team we all were and how proud I was to be part of it. This is a good example of what sets food service staff in Corrections apart from those folks working in most of the other areas of our industry. Talk about creating good PR; you can't do any better than that!

Most government agencies budget for food for training seminars, meetings and events. We created good PR by providing these services for quite a bit less than any outside entity. We charged them all of our costs including labor and still managed to save them money.

We had a great catering team, led by Food Service Supervisors Rene Panganiban and Neila Afan-Cook. As they always said, they didn't do this by themselves. Besides the main crew, including but not limited to, Alex, Rudy, Maggie, Bella, George, Sergio, Irenea, John, Erlinda, Doc and Myrna with Lynne and Adela decorating the special cakes, there were many more people at the Production Center who assisted as well.

We did such events as picnics for the Foster Child Parents and the Senior Sheriff Volunteers, training seminars for over 300 lawyers attached to the DA's office and the FBI and lunches for associations like the Southern California Jail Managers Association. We did great barbeques and outstanding Hawaiian Luaus. In many instances, the participants paid for their meals themselves and were happy to do so as the food was great; all we had was satisfied customers. Thank God; we wouldn't want to tick off the FBI or the DA, right?

One event stands out in my mind as the best one ever. We did a French Dinner for the grand opening of our new Central Jail which is still talked about today (in 2007) by some of those who attended. It was a fabulous seven course menu, all done in French, which started with Lemon-almond scallops and grilled marinated shrimp served with peach chutney and spicy cocktail sauce, garnished with mango and kiwi.

It ended with Bananas Foster Flambé over French vanilla bean ice cream. We used the original recipe which I received from the chef at Brennans Restaurant in New Orleans. We even had an ice sculpture of a mermaid as part of our decorations.

Of course, we hit a small snag. I sent the ice sculpture to be stored in a freezer that was not in a jail so the inmates wouldn't mess with it; I thought it would be safe. It arrived at the dinner site without the tip of one breast. (It was a discreet topless mermaid) It seems that one of the workers couldn't resist touching it and got stuck for a time to the sculpture; thus the missing tip. You can't make this stuff up!

Everyone was all upset but I told them we will make pasties for her. They all just looked at me and then looked at the floor, not knowing what to say. One of the Senior Cooks was already making floral arrangements out of vegetables and fruits which were gorgeous so he made the pasties and no one ever knew the difference.

CHEF RENE'S BBQ RIBS

This dish is simply fabulous!! Occasionally, we provided catering for various functions and these ribs were one of the most requested items. If we were doing an actual barbeque, we would put the ribs on the grill for a few minutes before the final cooking with the sauce to give them that charcoal flavor. I usually do not eat ribs but when I tested this recipe, I tasted them and kept eating!

Chef Rene Panganiban was a San Diego Sheriff's Food Service Supervisor and he was in charge of the catering program along with his regular duties. He never said no to any request and his culinary skills were second to none. We would meet and discuss the menu and when we would actually do the event, Rene always added his surprise special touches. I am so happy that I retired first as I would not have known what to do without him.

*Note: a word about the peppers in this dish. When I made this recipe, I put 1 teaspoon, about ½, of a yellow chili pepper in the sauce and it had a nice little kick. I do not like spicy things so if you do, put more peppers in the sauce.

Be careful how you cut the peppers. When I was cutting them, I protected my hands but I inhaled too deeply and choked for a while. How anyone puts that hot stuff in their mouth and enjoys it is beyond me. Also, you can use Jalapeno peppers but they are not as hot as the yellow ones so you will need a little more of them. I must confess I made the first batch of sauce without the hickory smoke flavoring as I could not find it at that time. Instead I used a tablespoon of hickory smoke flavored bottled BBQ Sauce. (Please, don't tell Rene) It was still wonderful! The sauce can be used for other dishes such as BBQ Chicken. I have since found the smoke flavoring and am following the recipe to the letter. (Honest, Rene)

Preheat oven to 450 degrees

Sauce:

- ½ medium tomato, chopped
- ½ medium onion, chopped
- *½ small yellow or Habaneras pepper, chopped fine
- 2 tablespoons vegetable or olive oil
- 1 cup tomato catsup
- ½ cup brown sugar
- ½ teaspoon hickory smoke flavoring
- 1 teaspoon molasses or soy sauce

Rub:

- 2 teaspoons chili powder
- 2 teaspoons garlic powder
- ½ teaspoon salt
- ½ teaspoon black pepper
- 3-4 pounds beef or pork ribs

1. In a skillet over medium heat, sauté the tomatoes, onions and chili peppers in the oil for 8-10 minutes, stirring frequently. Reduce the heat and add the catsup, brown sugar, hickory smoke flavoring and molasses. Let it simmer for 10 minutes, stirring constantly. (The sauce will be thick) Set aside off the heat.
2. Make the rub by combining the chili powder, garlic powder, salt and pepper.

3. Rub the ribs on both sides with the mixture.

4. Line a baking pan with tin foil. Place the ribs, bone side down, in the pan and cook in a 450 degree oven for ½ hour.

5. Remove the ribs from the oven and cover them with the BBQ Sauce. Cover tightly with more tinfoil.

6. Reduce the heat to 250 degrees and bake the ribs for 1 ¼ hours or until tender.

Chapter 16
Always Have Fun

A Cover for my License Plates:
Done working, alarm clock for sale.
You Are Only As Good As Your Last Meal!
Popular Food Service Truism

One of my mottos is "Always Have Fun". You should have a passion for whatever you do in life; it is extremely important you enjoy your work; you spend so much time doing it. I have helped employees by telling them that I can tell that they do not enjoy what they are doing. When they ask me how I know, I tell them that it is because they do not do it well; then we gave them a little help. It takes a special kind of person to work successfully in Corrections. Eventually, we had a team that did well in their work and loved every minute.

I had the good fortune to have two excellent assistants, Paul and Hans. Between them they had over fifty years of experience in managing large operations. They were not afraid to give me advice, opinions and their expertise to keep me from messing up. When we all agreed on the way to go, they went and got it done for which I am eternally grateful. They both retired a short time before I did and they were replaced by Ray Bullock and Kurt Greiner who did a good job for us as well.

I was blessed to have three executive secretaries over the years, Sharon, Elvie and Carol. They all did a fabulous job keeping me on the straight and narrow and making me look good. I don't know what I would have done without Mercy, my chief accountant. She was the backbone of our division, keeping the budget on course, the bills paid and managing millions of dollars like it was nothing. All the clerical staff did their jobs with professionalism and a smile.

We had wonderful skilled and dedicated cooks, senior cooks, food service workers and supervisors who worked hand in hand with our truck drivers and stock clerks, performing their duties at one thousand percent, making it happen each and every day.

I thoroughly enjoyed my time in jail; the people that I had the privilege to work with made it amazingly enjoyable and professionally rewarding. I owe everything I accomplished to all the fantastic members of my food service staff who practiced such professionalism every single day.

From my first commander who hired me and put up with all my new ideas to the last one, I was truly blessed. They empowered me to do my job and to make things happen, even though I know I must have driven them crazy at times. Thanks guys and gals! I don't even know how I will ever thank the best Sheriff ever; Sheriff Kolender. He empowered all of us to excel each and every day. They all enabled me to receive many awards, both from the San Diego Sheriff and the Food Service Industry.

I have belonged to the Association of Correctional Food Service Affiliates for 28 years; I had the honor to be the President-Elect and President from 1992-95. I want to thank all the members for the education and assistance I received over the years which helped me to achieve my goals and to those of you who donated recipes for this book.

The last award I received before retiring in 2007 was the Medal of Distinction from the California Peace Officers Association. I was one of only two women out of 40 people receiving awards that day and I really felt special. To receive this medal from a law enforcement organization was a huge honor and it meant a lot to me to receive it right when I retired from the Sheriff's Department.

On June 22, 2007, my staff gave me a wonderful retirement luncheon which was attended by over 200 people. It was beautifully organized by Mercy Cabico, our extraordinary chief accountant, Neila Afan-Cook, Rene Panganiban and so many others. Of course Sheriff Bill Kolender was there as well as the Undersheriff, Bill Gore, (who is now Sheriff), many of the commanders, Captains and deputies, professional staff managers, the Purchasing Director and other representatives of different County Departments and a representative from the County Board of Supervisors.

Of course, many of my staff members were there as well as my husband, children, grandchildren and friends. What a fabulous buffet they cooked for us that included all my favorites such as Prime Rib and shrimp, in addition to dozens of other dishes and a huge decorated cake with my picture on it. I had never seen anything like it.

There were many wonderful speeches; my husband Larry even got up and spoke and did such a great job, he received a standing ovation. My husband was always my chief sounding board and critic and helped me in many ways to achieve my goals. I received many beautiful gifts which I will always cherish. Everything given to me that day was from their hearts and it made me so very happy that it made me want to stay for a few more years. I couldn't help but think I was lucky to leave on a high note before I did something to mess it up. Remember, in food service we are "only as good as our last meal".

I was presented with a proclamation from the California Legislature "extolling my many achievements and extending the deep appreciation of the people of California" for my work. What an honor for *all of us* who work so hard every day in Correctional Food Service.

In addition, I received a proclamation from the County of San Diego, signed by the Vice Chairman, Greg Cox. In it they proclaimed June 22, 2007, to be "Louise E. Mathews Day" throughout San Diego County, commending me for, among other things, years of professionalism, dedication and commitment to the people of San Diego. I was blown away; a day named for me, a Sheriff Food Service Chief; what a tremendous honor!

Of course I had to inject a little humor into it so I wouldn't cry too much; I asked if this meant we could all get the day off with pay. All in all, it was a wonderful ending to a great career.

I hope you use some of the delicious recipes in this book to have your own Jail House Food Nights at home, from "the right side of the bars". I wish you Bon Appetite!

LOUISA'S FAMOUS RUM CAKE

After working hard in jails all day you can feel a little depressed as well as stressed to the max! What you need is a piece of "to die for" rum cake to help soothe your spirit. This is my recipe; notice how easy it is? It is a potent cake due to the fact that I do not burn off the alcohol.

I just lick the syrup pan and my legs start to go numb. This cake has been a hit no matter where I take it. If I am bringing something else to a pot luck affair, they tell me I have to bring this cake as well.

I brought it to a Les Dame d' Escoffier indoor picnic; this is a highly esteemed culinary organization for women. It was 100 degrees that day and the cake had started to disintegrate in the car. I kind of pushed it back together and placed it on a huge table filled with all these gorgeous desserts made by professional pastry chefs.

Believe it or not, everyone loved it and wanted the recipe. It appeared in the organization's magazine no less than 4 times and looked pretty good if I do say so myself. Of course, I had put the *falling apart* side pointing towards the middle of the filled table so no one ever knew the difference. Mama didn't raise no fool.

Preheat oven to 350 degrees

- 1 box Vanilla Cake Mix
- 2 cups pecan halves or walnut pieces
- 1 ½ cups rum(split)
- 1 cup granulated sugar

- 8 ounces (2 sticks) butter or margarine
- Powdered sugar for garnish
- 2 cups whole strawberries for garnish

1. Grease one Bundt pan and sprinkle ½ of the nuts in the pan.
2. Prepare the cake mix according to the directions on the box except replace a half cup of the water called for with a half cup of rum.
3. Pour the mixture into the Bundt pan; sprinkle the top with the rest of the nuts. Bake the cake at 350 degrees until moist crumbs appear on the toothpick. Remove the cake from the oven and poke holes in the hot cake with a long fork.
4. In the meantime, prepare the rum syrup. Melt the sugar and the butter together in a medium saucepan, stirring constantly to prevent burning. Cook over medium heat for two minutes. Remove from the stove and slowly add the remaining rum and stir. If you do it too fast, it will overflow the pan.
5. Slowly spoon the hot syrup over the top of the cake. Allow the cake to cool and then invert the cake onto a plate. Place cake in refrigerator and chill for at least two hours.
6. Before serving, sift powdered sugar all over the cake. Fill the center of the cake with the strawberries and garnish around the edges of the cake as well.
7. The cake can be served as is or with ice cream or whipped cream.
8. Keep the cake refrigerated until serving. Note: the longer the cake sits in the refrigerator, the more intensified the flavor of rum becomes. You will have to hide it well because everyone will be eating it.

Variations: Use a chocolate cake mix and add Kahlua everywhere the original recipe calls for rum. You can substitute Whiskey or Bourbon with a vanilla or lemon cake mix. They are all good! Enjoy!

Index of Recipes

Adobo Seasoning, 156

Alligator Stew, 121

Bangers and Mash, 154

BBQ Ribs, 169

Boosted Milk Shake, 92

Breads:

    Cramique (raisin breakfast bread), 43

    Indian Fry Bread, 143

    Tony's Salami Bread, 13

    Zucchini Bread, 28

Cakes:

    Carrot Cake, xiv

    Cheesecake ala Russo, 8

    Easy Chocolate Cake, 18

    Aunt Dolly's Crumb Cake, 11

    Lazy me Cake, 101

    Prune (High Energy) Cake, 40

    Rum Cake, 175

    Tea Cakes, 150

    Ugly Duckling Cake, 55

Chicken:

    Chicken Adobo, 54

    Miss Marie's Fried Chicken, 27

    Fried Chicken Fingers, 130

    Chicken Gizzard Stew, 109

    Gentse Waterzooi, 148

    Orange Glazed Chicken, 93

    Porto Rican Chicken and Rice, 158

    Southern Style Chicken Casserole, 115

    Thai Chicken Curry, 64

Chili Conquistador, 137

Cookies:
Potato Chip Cookies, 101
Ranger Cookies, 29
Creole Seasoning, 130
Desserts:
Banana Streusel Muffins, 89
Chocolate Chip Bread Pudding, 87
Aunt Jack's Awesome Brownies, 112
Fresh Fruit Dessert Pizza, 123
Maple Nut Sweet Buns, 52
Disciplinary Diet, 94
Frostings;
Mocha, 14
Steve's Cream Cheese Fudge, 14
Jail House Burrito, 126
Menudo, 142
Perogies, 153
Pie
English Pie Crust, 6
Lemon Chess, 119
Pizza Casserole, 127
Salads
Cathy's Corn Salad, 39
Sensational South African Rice Salad, 100
Tomato Aspic Salad, 116
Sauces:
Pork and Tomato Gravy, 9
Sweet and Sour, 20
Sofrito, 156

Soups:

    Cream of Broccoli, xiii

    Mr. Z's Fish Chowder, 83

    Lentils and Rice, 152

    Cream of Peanut, 120

    Pozole, 133

Tilapia Jambalaya, 105

Turkey Noodle Casserole, 135

Vegetables/Side Dishes:

    Beans Charros, 140

    Red Beans and Sausage, 107

    Broccoli Cheese Bake, 139

    Collard Greens with Ham Hocks, 113

    Cranberry Relish, 114

    Fried Grits, 111

    Rice and Pigeon Peas, 157

    Spanish Rice, 66

About the Author

Louise Mathews has 43 years experience in Food Service Management in Hotels, Schools, Hospitals, and Large-Scale Restaurants. She spent the last 21 years as the San Diego Sheriff's Chief of Food and Nutrition Services. In this capacity she designed a 43,000 square foot Production Center, the first of its kind in Corrections, and operated it for 17 years before retiring in 2007. It produced 42,000 meals per day, supplying meals to 8200 people per day; over 10 million meals per year. In addition, Louise Mathews has 20 years experience as a Food Service Management, Design and Operational Consultant as President of L&M Consulting. In this capacity she assisted in the design and operation of many other Production Centers including those in New Orleans, Louisiana, Alameda, California, Montana State Prison, Toronto, Canada, Cook County, Chicago and the Marine Corps Facility in Japan. She is an acknowledged expert in the use of Cook/Chill Technology, large scale Bakeries, and the Correctional Market.

Among Louise Mathews' professional organizations are the Association of Correctional Food Service Affiliates, the Silver Plate Society, the Les Dames D' Escoffier International, Read San Diego and the Publishers/Writers Group of San Diego. She has lectured at San Diego State University and St. Vincent De Paul's and she is the PAC Committee Emeritus for the San Diego Art Institute's Culinary Program.

Louise Mathews has received many awards, including: the Silver Plate Award, 1994, Honorary Doctorate of Food Service Degree, 1995, Honor Medal of Merit, San Diego Sheriff's Department, 1995, the American Correctional Food Service Association's Operator of the Year Award, 1998, the International Diamond Award, Best Food Service in Corrections, 2001, the International Sapphire Award, Best Food Service Director, 2002, the Outstanding Employee Award, San

Diego County Sheriff's Department, 2005-2006 and the Medal of Distinction, California Peace Officers Association, 2007. Upon her retirement from the San Diego Sheriff's Department, she was presented with a Proclamation from the California Legislature for her 21 years of leadership, superb technical skills and professional competence. In addition, the San Diego Board of Supervisors presented her with a Proclamation declaring June 22, 2007, as Louise E. Mathews' Day in acknowledgement of her 21 years of dedication and excellent service to the people of the County of San Diego.